MW00941761

MY APPALACHIAN TRIAL I

THREE WEDDINGS AND A SABBATICAL

STEVE ADAMS

My Appalachian Trial I: Three Weddings and a Sabbatical

by

Steve Adams

Copyright © 2016 by Steve Adams. All rights reserved.
Reproduction in whole or part of this publication without
express written consent is strictly prohibited.

Please visit:

www.steveadams.info

About the Author

It took me over 40 years in the insurance industry to come to the conclusion that life could—and should—be better. I decided that climbing mountains, walking through forests, living like a hobo, then writing about my experiences would be a lot more fun. The publication of these two volumes has taken a lot of time, energy, and self-examination that I have enjoyed immensely. Added to that enjoyment is the realization that I can articulate my thoughts and put them into these pages. My  writing career is in its early stages and I hope that you want to join me in this and other adventures in the future.

As always, my lovely wife, Diane, will be with me every step of the way at our home in sunny Florida.

Acknowledgments

Any book, however intimate, is a collaborative process. When I was writing, I was entirely responsible for everything that appeared on my laptop. Once those long, lonely days were over, the true job of a writer came into focus. I canvassed several friends, listened to countless podcasts, and read innumerable articles about the current state of the publishing industry.

All the advice I received led me to the need for a serious, professional editor and a book cover designer. My editor—suggested by a fellow hiker and author—was Liz Coursen. She introduced me to the concept of American English. This was a concept that I initially resisted. However, as I progressed through the editing process, a lot of it made sense and I buckled under her pressure. I believe, and I hope, that Liz has helped make this a better read than it was. Any remaining mistakes are mine, as is the occasional bad language.

I had the title in my head from the very beginning, although it was originally intended to be just one book. Consequently, the decision to split it into two volumes meant that I needed something other than "I" and "II" as differentiators. In this social media world, I naturally turned to Facebook to enlist help in coming up with sub-titles. I couldn't have been more delighted when my son, Rob, suggested those chosen.

I really love the covers of these two books, so additional thanks goes to Wootikom Hanroog. He understood what I wanted and patiently altered the design until I was happy. I found him through 99Designs, so kudos to them.

Two last shout-outs. First, the Appalachian Trail Class of 2014. I met many people on this journey, very few of whom I would have met had we not been dreamers. I've mentioned some and left out others, but there wasn't a single person I met who didn't have some impact upon my hike. Most of this impact was beneficial, though I'm sure that, even now, we are all still working out what this has meant to us. In some ways, I hope we never find out and retain that magic.

Last—but certainly most—I want to thank Diane for leaving me to pursue not only my hiking dream but also my writing dream when I returned home. I hope that I have made her proud of me.

Steve Adams
April 2016

This book is dedicated to my wife, Diane. I never needed her permission to take this trip, but I always needed her buy-in. There is a significant difference, and I will forever be grateful to her for understanding that.

Contents

Chapter 1: At The Top of Springer Mountain

It was late March. I was in the woods, just beyond the summit of Springer Mountain, Georgia, and about to do something I'd never done before. While there were many things that would became "firsts" over the next six months, this was to become my first night camping in my new tent or, indeed, in any tent, on my new sleeping pad and in my new quilt, on the very first hike of my life. For a night of so many firsts, I was surprisingly calm.

I looked around, perhaps a little too surreptitiously, as I took in both my new surroundings and my fellow hikers. I was trying to appear as nonchalant as possible, even though my hiking experience to this point amounted to a somewhat unimpressive total of eight miles. I was at the Springer Mountain Shelter, just 350 yards down and past the summit of the southern terminus of the Appalachian Trail. This was to be my baptism into camping in a tent, and I didn't want to blow it.

My choice of tent was, primarily, decided with this precise moment in mind. A few months earlier, while I'd been accumulating all my equipment for my adventure, I had thought carefully about how I'd feel at this very moment. I knew that I'd be with other people and that we would be settling down for our first night. We would be measuring up our companions, and probably judging how everybody else was faring. As a complete novice, I just wanted to get through it without appearing to be totally hopeless and somebody to avoid. Plus, as a Brit, I didn't want to make a complete prick of myself. I'm sorry, that's just how we are.

To that end, I had chosen a tent that would, in theory, be easy to erect and easy to disassemble. I had read review upon review of all the likely candidates, and had settled upon a Tarptent Rainbow. The big attraction for me was that this tent had a single, collapsible strut that would obviate the need to attach things to other things, a mystical skill that I do not possess, being about as impractical as a man can get. Tarptent even provides a helpful video on its website that shows a guy assembling his tent in about three minutes, so I was moderately confident that, given a fair wind, no rain, and limited interruptions, I could achieve the task in about 20 minutes. Such were my low, though entirely justifiable, expectations at this early stage.

What I hadn't considered was exactly *where* to pitch my temporary home. This oversight proved to be something of a schoolboy error that I paid for over the next couple of days. Nobody had mentioned the need to find as flat an area as possible, and, even though this should have been obvious, I paid scant regard to the spot I had chosen. I gratefully found a small clearing into which I incorporated myself amongst a growing overnight community.

I tipped the contents of my tent's stuff sack onto the ground, and, as coolly as I could manage, separated the folding strut from the tent itself, putting it together as if I'd been doing it all my life.

Having watched the tent assembly video at least 40 times, I was confident that I had it all down. Amazingly, I was staring, almost stupefied, at a completed tent less than five minutes later. I even checked it a few times to see if I'd left something out, and I must guiltily confess to a rather smug smile when I saw others struggling far more than I had. While it was a touch premature to consider myself a hiker, I certainly felt that I had successfully negotiated my first test. Tripping slightly over the guy ropes as I circled the tent didn't do much for my manly, competent image, but I regained my composure without too many people noticing.

To be frank, I wasn't actually sure about what to do next, so I sat on the ground and shot a video of myself in my new surroundings to allow myself to consider my options. A selfie as a defense mechanism is an interesting concept, though one that served me well more times than I should admit.

It seemed that others were now shoving things into their tents, and I suddenly became aware that I was supposed to share my tent with my 42-lb backpack. Who knew? Certainly not me, and it dawned upon me that it might have been sensible to have paid attention to the "best buy" designation on the Tarptent *Double* Rainbow when I had been looking at all the reviews. My reasoning for a one-man tent had been fairly straightforward, in that I had no intention of sharing the tent with anybody, so why get one with more space? The thought of where my backpack was going to spend the night simply had not crossed my mind.

It is worth pointing out here that when I referred previously to my eight miles of hiking experience, that had all been achieved earlier in the day, in my hike up the Springer Mountain Approach Trail from Amicolola Falls. I was literally a non-hiker until this very day and the various protocols that you learn regarding long-distance hiking can only really be acquired by actually hiking. Consequently, sharing my tent with my pack was a new concept that needed to be taken on board.

This realization changed everything. The tent had seemed tolerably roomy, even capacious, when I had set it up in my living room a week or so before. While that could hardly be described as field conditions, the flatness of my living room floor was a given, and thus never entered my calculations when locating a spot to camp.

Full disclosure: I had gone on a short walk of about three miles, two weeks prior to the start of my adventure, in a local state park in Florida. This was so that I could test carrying my loaded backpack, as well as continue breaking in my new boots. As you'd imagine, Florida state parks offer marginally greater inclines than my living room floor, though not by too much. That said, it made sense to set up the tent, if only to see if I could do it.

In the way of the British, I felt self-conscious when I got to an apparent campsite, for others had set up their tents already. These were real hikers and I felt very much a fraud as I set down my pack. Naturally enough, I sat there thinking about my next move. Sitting down prior to action of almost any kind became something of a motif for me in the months to come, a sort of breather to take stock, however insignificant the next task might be. After ten minutes of looking, I thought, singularly cool, I stood and went about my business. Nobody was paying any attention to me, so it seemed as good a time as any to get on with it.

As it did at the top of Springer, a couple of weeks later, the whole enterprise went off rather well. Once set up, I burrowed into my new temporary home, and, with nothing else inside the tent, there was plenty of room. Having sat upright for about two minutes, I re-emerged into the blinding heat, sweat pouring off me. Sitting inside a tent on a hot Florida day tends to do that to you, and this was only the middle of March. I had dark thoughts about how things might be in the height of summer in Virginia.

So that was it. The one and only time I'd properly put up the tent prior to the real thing, and the thought never struck me that I'd have a 40-pound companion. I felt as if I'd brought along an unexpected, recalcitrant child to sullenly share my adventure.

Back to the Springer Mountain Shelter, and having contemplated life for about five minutes, I was now openly watching what went inside the tent and what remained outside. I'm not sure how long it took for me to develop this habit, but I seem to recollect that it was fairly early that I came up with the following routine: first, I pitched my tent, normally with stakes, though sometimes with trekking poles at either end instead of stakes. The latter method was normally when there were wooden tenting platforms, so it was certainly pitched with stakes most of the time and definitely for the first couple of months.

I incorporated finding a flat spot into my tent-pitching routine after two or three nights. It became an absolute priority after sliding around in the middle of the night and finding myself in a pile at the lowest point of the tent on the first couple of mornings. A combination of failure and excruciating discomfort is the best way to learn the right way to do stuff, though I remained generally poor at this skill for the duration of my hike.

Second, I extracted my sleeping gear from the bottom compartment of my backpack and separated the individual items. I had chosen a quilt from Katabatic Gear, as opposed to a sleeping bag, and this necessitated a sleeping pad onto which the quilt fitted with a couple of strings. Despite this overload of detail to one such as me, it worked out remarkably well.

The big problem with the pad, however, was the need to inflate the darn thing. This quickly became one of the worst parts of my day. I constantly wished that I had invested in an inflator to allow my already over-extended lungs to finish the day without an extra, brain-giddying effort. You may think I'm exaggerating how much of a pain this became, but it truly struck me every night as I huffed and puffed my way to inflated comfort. You may also be wondering why I didn't rectify this omission at an early stage. Truth be told, I have no sensible answer. Having no sensible answer became another of my motifs on the trail.

Once done, I carefully unzipped the tent's bug net to push the pad into the tent, then quickly zipped it back up, irrationally fearful of bugs—or worse—joining me for the night. I then gathered my quilt, my quilt liner and my tent inner "ceiling," unzipped the bug net again, threw everything to the top end of the pad and re-zipped once more. Next, I rummaged around in my pack for my headlamp and my iPad, before repeating the zip and unzip process and leaving these items handy for the night.

Food was always a big part of camping, so the items related to my laughable culinary skills would be extracted next. A Jetboil Flash was my chosen camp stove, while my water was generally contained in a Nalgene bottle, so that joined the Jetboil. Then the food bag, later to become two food bags, as my wife attempted to fatten me up after some early catastrophic weight loss. Lastly, my bowl, my cup, and my spork would make up this growing pile.

When everything was out of the pack, a last unzip and zip would secure the pack in my tent and I was ready to eat.

The final part of this housekeeping jigsaw puzzle was the need to make sure that, after you had eaten, you didn't spend the night sleeping with your food bag inside your tent. Apparently, this was to avoid the unwanted company of a bear who might regard your food as something to be plundered, and, if you happened to get in the way of the plundering, well, tough.

I'd paid close attention to this aspect of the routine and was happy to see that, in Georgia, bear cables were provided at shelters for the use of hikers. These cables are a type of pulley system—attached between sturdy trees—that can be lowered to enable the hiker to add his pack or food bag to a carabiner before pulling the whole thing aloft.

So, there I was, an hour or so later, having eaten and chatted with my new friends, with my food bag blowing gaily in the breeze, 15 feet above the ground. I was ready for bed, and, frankly, exhausted by the maelstrom of thoughts competing for primacy in my head. I was about to hike the Appalachian Trail, and, probably a touch too late, I wondered how I got there.

Chapter 2: The Whys and the Wherefores

Living in England for the majority of my 61 years, I was blissfully unaware of even the existence of the Appalachian Trail, let alone harbor a desire to hike it. I was a city boy, working all my life up to that point in London, in the insurance industry. I was very well traveled in the way of mid- to high-level insurance executives, seeing hotels, offices, airports, and bars, though rarely in that order. I was something of a voracious reader at the time, especially when flying. I would devour all sorts of books that would catch my fancy, normally at the airport, generally buying them on impulse.

Bill Bryson is an American author who was living and writing in the U.K. at that time, contributing columns to a British newspaper. He was a writer I had come to admire. I always found his columns to be funny and well-researched, often sharing dazzling facts with his readers, facts that would embed themselves in my brain.

A Walk in the Woods was published in 1998, a time that saw me travel extensively in my job, and I grabbed a copy one day as I was about to board a plane. Japan and Australia were regular destinations for me in the late 90s, so it is likely that it was on one of these trips that I got stuck into my new book. While I am not certain as to where I was going, I know that I was immediately hooked by Bryson's revelation of a place beyond my experience. It wasn't that his story was particularly gripping or his descriptions were so vivid; I was more intrigued by the concept of a trail that took the hiker from the south of the United States all the way to the very north. Bryson described his journey with his friend, Katz, in laugh-out-loud anecdotes. The two of them were having an adventure, and what boy, whatever his age, can resist an adventure?

I soon learned on the trail that A.T. hikers are divided over Bryson and his book, some reflecting that his experience does not illustrate the trail as it is, while others, me included, take his story for what it is. He wrote his story, about his hike, and that certainly inspired me and, speaking with people I met on the trail, many others as well. You'd be surprised how vitriolic some people became at even the mention of Bryson's name; it was one of the few ugly sides of people's characters that I noticed on the trail, and one out of all proportion to his supposed crime.

Hike Your Own Hike, or HYOH, is probably the number one tenet of the Appalachian Trail and one that I quickly came to respect. This is because there are so many ways in which the A.T. can be tackled to make it an experience to suit each hiker. Slackpacking was something that I heard about at an early stage. Hostels would often offer the service to enhance their own business, taking groups or individuals to a convenient point somewhere further along the trail. The hiker, or hikers, would then trek back towards the previous stopping point, then return to the hostel for a second, even third, night. The great benefit in slackpacking was the lighter pack that was needed for these days. Often, a day pack was sufficient, with just water and food. When you have been carrying a 40-lb slab on your back for several weeks or months, a 30-lb relief feels deliriously lighter.

Another alternative was "yellow blazing," so-named after the yellow lines on the roads that intersect the A.T. Some hikers chose to avoid one or two of the tougher mountains by hitching into nearby towns, before resuming their hike from that town. This would normally entail missing a few miles of the Appalachian Trail.

There are purists for whom it is anathema to slackpack, or to "yellow blaze," yet I can't overstate just how tedious such fundamentalism becomes—as does pretty much every kind of fundamentalism, now that I think of it. We all come to the trail from different directions and we all have our own reasons for making this journey. Who is anybody to criticize another's purpose or another's method? For me, I was determined to hike every step and to pass every blaze; however, I embraced the concept of slackpacking near the end like a junkie in an Ibizan nightclub, and I earned my Katahdin picture and A.T.C. certificate because I achieved them on my terms. Others will have carried every pound every step of the way and good for them. Several people missed out a few mountaintops and a few miles—the yellow blazers—but I certainly don't begrudge them the same picture and certificate that I have. We're all there for the journey and there is no one "right" way.

Once the thought of the trail was in my head, I just couldn't shake it, propelling it straight to the top of my Bucket List. For me, this was an imaginary list of things that I'd like to do at some indeterminate point in my life. At the same time, I was fully aware that I was never likely to return seriously to the list to accomplish any of them. I suppose it is a human frailty to want to do something so apparently out of reach, and, once I'd set up my Bucket List, there was never anything else to usurp the A.T. I let it stew for about 15 years and, when the opportunity presented itself, I grabbed it. I had never forgotten the excitement I felt at the prospect of such a journey, and I reflected that it is only when the stars align that some ambitions become attainable.

I didn't know it at the time, but my stars were already shifting into place.

That I was living and working full time in England and shortly to end my second marriage may have had something to do with my feeling that this would be an impossible endeavor. The fact that I wasn't the least bit interested in hiking for the sake of hiking may also have played a part. While I've loved and participated in many sports over the years, "outdoorsy" wouldn't be a term with which even my most ardent admirer would label me. That term conjures, for me, images of square-jawed men, with ham-like, ludicrously hairy forearms that emerge from the rolled-up sleeves of plaid shirts, tackling unspeakable hardships in wild, harsh places in the frozen north. I'm not that guy; I'm absolutely nothing like that guy. Mind you, as I was to learn on my adventure, neither were many, if any, of the people with whom I shared the Appalachian Trail in 2014. In so many ways, the vast majority of my pre-conceived ideas of what the trail would be like were entirely incorrect. Even starting from zero experience, I soon realized that the only way that one can become experienced in hiking this and, I suspect, other trails, is to simply go ahead and do it. Further, I'd suggest that it was my lack of any hiking bad habits that enabled me to modify behaviors to make my hike better as each situation arose.

The U.K. has many trails and I hadn't been moved to attempt any of those, so what was it about the A.T. that made it so tempting and kept a fire burning within me for so many years, despite being a non-hiker?

The facts alone were sufficiently daunting to put off most people. The 2014 trail—the length changes each year—stretched for 2,185.3 miles, covered 14 states, and was estimated to take about 5,000,000 steps to complete. I found it difficult to put that distance into context, though a conversation with my sister-in-law Suzy allowed me at least some yardstick by which to measure it. About three months before I left, she had been speaking with me about my plans. When I mentioned the mileage, she asked me more about it. Pausing for a second, I replied, "Imagine driving from your home in Brooklyn, all the way down I-95 to your folks' place in Orlando, then turning straight around and driving all the way back to Brooklyn. However, instead of taking I-95, I'll be going over mountains and foot-wide pathways the whole way."

We looked at each other in awe, taking in what I had just said. We'd both made that drive and it had seemed endless, yet I was planning the substantially more scenic route with a 40-lb pack on my back. I also pointed out that there was an elevation gain of the equivalent of 16 times the height of Mount Everest, so my "going over mountains" had been something of an understatement.

I'm not sure who was the more dumbstruck by this articulation of the task ahead, me or Suzy. Nobody had put it to me in these terms before. I'd just blurted them out, but the awfulness of it stuck with me for days afterward. Suddenly, seeing the distance and difficulty in these terms allowed me the context I'd been searching for and the result was stultifying.

We all know what walking five miles would be like, and I guess we could all imagine what walking 20 miles would be like, but this number was so out of reach as to be impossible to imagine. Seeing this as I'd expressed it, I wondered if I had any realistic chance of even getting out of Georgia, let alone making it all the way to Maine. The next few weeks were spent trying to nullify those doubts, as I went about choosing my gear and preparing to leave.

The length of the walk wasn't my only concern, of course; I had a long list of worries that were piling up the whole time. There is nothing like a deadline, or, in my case, an imminent departure date, to bring problems into focus.

I was concerned about all manner of wildlife, including—in no particular order of buttock-clenching fear—bears, snakes, moose, wild boar, and even the fabled mountain lion. Of all these delights, it was the bear that was mainly exercising my brain. Everything I had read should have convinced me that bears weren't the least bit interested in eating humans and that they would, in nearly every case, run away. I knew that coming between a mama bear and her young might cause some consternation, but that was something I would try to avoid at all costs.

However, the nagging fear remained that, for fairly obvious reasons, bears hadn't read the books that I had, and, given the slightest opportunity, would treat me as a succulent, if rather fatty, steak to be savored. For the first couple of weeks on the trail, I would see every burned-out tree and misshapen rock as a potential bear, as I scoured the path ahead, waiting for some movement to confirm my fears.

These early worries were, of course, groundless. Indeed, I soon acquired an eagerness to actually see a bear. This desire was increased by the day, as none were forthcoming. It would be a long time before that desire was satisfied.

Moving on from the spectacular mileage and the imaginary carnivorous nature of my fellow forest dwellers, I now focused on the expectation that a thru-hiker will take about five million steps completing his or her Georgia-to-Maine meander. The number itself also had concerns for me, especially once I was underway.

A quick-and-dirty calculation revealed that each step should thus average about 2.3 feet. I was hotly disputing this conclusion early on, as I staggered slowly uphill, barely able to breathe, planting each foot marginally in front of the other, making sluggish, even slug-like, progress. On the descent it was far easier to breathe, though I'd have had to leap like a gazelle if I was going to maintain an average of 2.3 feet. That wasn't happening, because the downhills were all about preventing your knees from disintegrating beneath you. Consequently, I gave up on the five million steps at an early stage, believing that it would likely be nearer to seven or eight million.

Age was also an issue that kept me awake at night.

I was a passably fit, though decidedly chunky, 61-year-old man when I approached this hike. Let me tell you, that is not the optimum age for the Appalachian Trail. Most of the people with whom I came into contact were in their 20s or late teens, many choosing to use the six months after, or before, college as a kind of interregnum prior to getting down to their real lives.

As an aside, it was very noticeable during the hike that the definition of "real" life became somewhat blurred, even for those of us no longer trying to define who or what we were.

I can't be sure what percentage of the hikers in 2014 were in the younger category, though the Appalachian Trail Conservancy came up with "more than 50 percent," which appeared to be woefully inaccurate. I'd have put the figure nearer 75 or 80 percent.

The statistic that captured my imagination more than any other, however, was that there had been fewer than 500 completions by hikers over 60 years of age. Ever! Now that was a number to ponder. It was such a small proportion of all thru-hikers that it seemed to me to be a very elite group worth joining, and I hung on to that thought throughout the trail. Mind you, the pessimist may have thought that such a low number would work against me being able to complete the trail. I, on the other hand, would see it as a badge of honor to be achieved. My glass-half-full attitude has generally served me well most of my life, as I have always been far more confident in my own abilities than any achievements should have merited.

As an example, I'm the type of golfer who, when coming to the last hole, having played like a drain all day long, still believes that he can bend a ball 220 yards out of the rough, around a tree, and onto the green. My unerring confidence in my own ability can come across as more than a touch arrogant sometimes. For the trail it was a very important component of my hiking psyche and allowed me to overcome difficult times that lay ahead. After all, I reasoned, I'm just going for a walk.

Chapter 3: Becoming Mighty Blue

It seems appropriate, given my admission to more than a sliver of arrogance in my make-up, that I should mention my self-imposed trail name and its origins.

This was another early concern for me, in that I didn't want to give some spotty oik the opportunity to give me a name that made him laugh and me squirm. I was eager to come up with something that I could live with for the duration of my hike. Being referred to as "England" or "Mr. Bean" or any other unexciting English derivation, would have driven me crazy, so choosing my own name was critical. I've found over the years that if you leave things to chance, chance will generally take great delight in spitting in your face and screwing you over.

I was looking for a combination that contained sufficient British self-deprecation, along with something that might provoke conversation. My initial attempt, mainly championed by Diane, my wife, was "King." Of course, this would have done nothing to avert the arrogance charge; in fact, it may well have confirmed it, and that is what eventually made me think further. However, the reason I had chosen King in the first place was far more prosaic than it might appear.

I'd been in insurance all my life and was attending a life insurance seminar in Florida when the presenter asked a question of the class. Seeing that nobody else was stepping forward, I put up my hand and spoke. You'd have thought that a multi-headed alien had landed. Everybody looked at me as if subtitles were required. The presenter, a self-styled Southern Cracker, shouted out, "You sound like the King!" Now, if you've ever heard me speak, I clearly don't sound like the King. Not only do we not have a King in the U.K., my accent is generally regarded as one of the less-aristocratic accents. No King, were we to have one, would be caught dead speaking like me.

Diane liked that story, so King it was. I even presented myself as such in my blog and was moving forward with it, even though I had some misgivings about the arrogance bit.

A few weeks later, when I was in a closet looking for some clothes to wear on the trail, I came across a shirt I'd bought the previous year. It was a team shirt of my favorite soccer team in the U.K. When I say my favorite soccer team, I am spectacularly understating the love I have for this team. If you've ever seen the English Premier League (and, by the way, it is football and not soccer everywhere other than in the U.S.), you will probably have noticed the rabid devotion that the fans express on behalf of their teams. Such fervor is something ingrained from early childhood, with fathers taking their sons and imbuing them with their own passion for the local team.

Thus it was with me and my father, as I started going to see Southend United with him in 1959. Southend was my hometown, on the coast, 40 miles east of London, and had been a favorite resort destination of the poor in East London for over a century. The town hosts the longest pleasure pier in the world, though the pier has burned so often that the pleasure designation is merely nominal these days.

Southend United was always one of the lower-league teams and never had any significant success. The club fluctuated sporadically through the divisions and briefly got into the league just below what is now the Premier League in the early '90s. Almost inexplicably, in light of an unbroken spell of 70 years of woeful performances, Southend fans started referring to their habitually hapless team as the Mighty Blues. The team played in blue shirts, so that at least was fair enough, but mighty? I think not. Still, there is nothing like the blind optimism and slavish devotion of the English soccer fan, so the Mighty Blues they became.

Grabbing the team shirt, I immediately decided that Mighty Blue could be the only possible name for me and instantly adopted it. I was a hapless hiker and I wore blue. Check, and double-check.

Now that I had the name, I started trying to wear it. I've always been Steve, not Stephen—other than to my mother—and giving myself a new name needed a further change to cement it.

I had considered shaving my head for the duration of the trip, though I hadn't actually done anything about it. However, in the ten or so days prior to leaving, I was starting to get more than a little nervous about what I was doing.

As I mentioned earlier, I was very much a hiking virgin, but I was about to embark upon an adventure for which I was demonstrably unprepared. Consequently, I felt that I needed something to kick-start the hike for me so, with just about a week to go, I firmly decided upon the new, shiny look. I'd always been something of a silver fox, with a politician's hair—though none of the diplomatic skills—so losing my hair was quite a meaningful thing for me. I decided that my normal hairdresser wouldn't be right for this, as she basically trimmed and rearranged my hair. It must be said, though, that she did look rather fetching in the mirror.

I selected a local, old-school barber shop, where Wendell, the proprietor, shaves heads and applies hot towels. I had to wait until two days before leaving for Atlanta, because I went back to the U.K. the weekend before departure to say goodbye to friends and family. Needless to say, I took in a Mighty Blues game at the same time. So, with the decision made and my nerves fraying, I went with Diane to get it done. The whole thing was over in about 35 minutes, even though 90 percent of the hair was gone in a few seconds, putting a change of mind beyond the realms of possibility. One of the problems of getting your hair cut in front of a mirror is that it is, literally, in your face, and I stared at a person who wasn't me anymore. Diane and Wendell were suddenly talking with somebody new, so radical was the change. When it was over, I waded through the remnants of my luxuriant mane, now lying on the floor, and emerged into the bright sunshine.

At that moment, I felt totally calm and all my previous fears melted away. I'd gone into the barber shop as Steve, and was now Mighty Blue, having put Steve to one side. I was walking away from my marriage into an adventure that would have a profound effect upon me over the next six months and beyond.

Friday morning, March 21, was the day we had chosen to fly to Atlanta. Even though I had been against it originally, I was glad that Diane was coming with me. While I wanted to get going with the trip, I hadn't managed to extricate myself emotionally from her, something I felt the need to do to reflect our upcoming geographical separation.

We were relative newlyweds, having married in the exotic Turks and Caicos Islands less than six years before. I was something of a serial bridegroom, with two ex-wives to my name, while Diane had married me as her first and only husband, so this wasn't easy for either of us.

I'd originally moved from London to New York in 2005 with a very sweet girlfriend, Jacinta. She had—rashly, in retrospect—trusted in our future so much that she had sold her thriving hairdressing business in London. I was working long hours and drinking far more than was strictly necessary, while she was unable to work due to her visa restrictions. These circumstances made for a very unhappy time for both of us, but mainly her, for I was regularly anesthetized with wine or vodka, often both.

As we gradually drifted apart, I returned with her to London to visit friends in late November 2005 and left her there, returning as a single man to New York. When you've been divorced twice and another relationship hits the rocks, you are long past the stage of blaming others for this modern take on Musical Chairs. I had behaved deplorably and I knew it.

Being single in New York, however, is certainly something to experience at least once in your life, though preferably when you actually are single. That is even more the case when you have your fair share of cash, live in a great apartment overlooking the Hudson River, are scrupulously clean, and are tolerably good-looking, or at least aren't so ugly as to frighten children and animals.

Even being in my early 50s didn't disqualify me from entering the New York dating scene, since I possessed that most sought-after of traits—a genuine English accent. As I mentioned earlier, this wasn't the cut-glass English accent of royalty, yet it still transcended all barriers. I found myself constantly in demand. With the additional help of such online dating sites as Match.com, I was rarely at home.

That said, it tended to lead to a confusing, barren imitation of life that missed out on all the good parts of dating. Once you made contact online and exchanged a few details via email, then talked on the phone, your first actual date felt more like a third date. If there was a second date, it was like a fifth date, and the whole process moved forward at breakneck speed towards an inevitable consummation. There was little real interaction to precede that dreadful moment of waking up next to somebody with whom you were casually acquainted and with whom you had likely shared more bodily fluids than words.

It was never like that with Diane.

She had worked with an old friend of mine—also Steve—25 years previously, and had discovered his new workplace through a casual conversation with mutual friends one evening. Steve had married and had a couple of children, so the two of them met and had a few drinks as buddies. The following morning, Steve called and told me, "I've just met the perfect woman for you. She is as gorgeous now as she was 25 years ago. She's never married, never had kids or even lived with anybody and, most important of all, she won't put up with any of your bullshit." This seemed a touch harsh, though not entirely unfair, so I let it slide without comment.

I was a larger-than-life figure, with a rash tendency to speak considerably in advance of engaging my brain, coupled with an alcoholic intake that exacerbated that tendency. Somebody once asked me if I did, in fact, think before speaking.

I replied that what I was thinking sounded so much better in my thoughts than it sounded once the thought left my mouth.

Steve had correctly spotted that Diane would not put up with somebody like me. That said, he knew me well enough to be aware of some of my better qualities and thought we'd make a great couple. He even said as much to Diane and, hearing this, she apparently dismissed me out of hand, inquiring as to why she would be interested in meeting a womanizing Brit who was a boozer, and who was living with somebody else. Steve recalls that the sentence was a little more graphic than that, but I think he caught the flavor. To be fair, she had a point that I would have found difficult to argue with. So there you have it. I was clearly a less-than-appetizing prospect for Diane and we would never meet.

Time moved on, Jacinta had returned to London, and I indulged myself in as much of the local dating scene as possible. I was dating women 20 years younger and, occasionally, several years older. Steve and I met several times over lunch, plotting to engineer a meeting between Diane and me. Hard though it was for old friends to believe, I was starting to tire of this duplicitous and hedonistic lifestyle and wanted something, or somebody, of substance in my life.

Steve managed to fix a drink with Diane in a bar just outside Grand Central Station, asking her if she would mind if an old friend joined them. I believe he was a bit hazy as to who that friend would be. She had apparently expunged the drunken Brit from her mind, and I showed up after they had both treated themselves fairly liberally to the cocktail menu.

We hit it off straightaway and, with the evening going so well, I suggested dinner, for the three of us, in the Oyster Bar inside the station. Suddenly, I wasn't playing any more. I knew instinctively that this was somebody who would test me and make me work for her affections more than anyone I had met.

A chaste peck on the cheek was reward enough at the end of the evening and I pursued her from that day. For a variety of reasons, we were unable to get together for about six weeks after our first drink, though we remained in touch via email and maybe the occasional phone call. Eventually, I was able to meet her for brunch and, even though we had a great time, events conspired once more to keep us apart.

At the end of September, and about four months after we had first met, I returned from a trip to Spain. I invited Diane for dinner at my apartment. From that day, we were almost inseparable, marrying 14 months later.

So, six years after our beautiful wedding, I was flying out of her life and, by a neat irony, we were even separated on the plane. Diane was sitting in the row in front of me. It seemed fitting somehow, and, as we landed in Atlanta, I was already walking away from her.

My newfound calmness had settled on me and, while we drove north in a rental car from Atlanta, I continued the transition. I was steeling myself for the physical separation that would take place the following day. I'm sure Diane realized this was happening, but nothing was said.

Luckily, we had the afternoon and evening ahead of us. We had booked a hotel just outside the beautiful village of Dahlonega, only 17 miles from Amicalola Falls State Park, my intended start point. Wandering around the stores, in and out of bookshops and places that sold trinkets for the home, we captured a little normalcy, though the parting the following day hung over us like Damocles' sword.

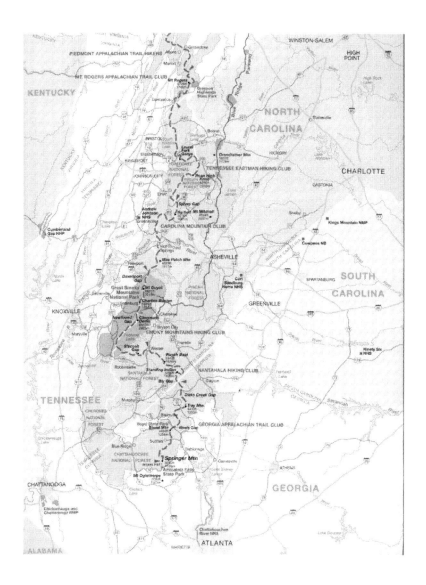

Chapter 4: First steps

Waking after a fitful sleep on that Saturday morning, we headed straight for the state park, planning on a last breakfast together at the lodge. The drive was quiet, with desultory conversation trying, but failing, to cover our unexpressed thoughts.

Looking out of the window at the lodge, while I sat devouring eggs, bacon, and all the trimmings, I could see how close we were to the wilderness. Everything looked cold and lonely out there and I was going into it willingly. Diane would have to get used to the fact that by nightfall—and many nights after—I would be camping out in this bleak place. That feeling was one that she never fully came to terms with for my entire time on the trail. We could both feel the pull of separation as we left the lodge. My backpack was full, having been augmented by a delivery of food that Diane had mailed to our hotel, and I was ready to go.

Amicalola Falls State Park is the launch point for many Appalachian Trail thru-hikers, with an office near the entrance for northbound hikers—NOBOs—to register their intended hike. Registration requested hikers to submit the date, their real name, a trail name, an intended destination, and their pack weight. There is a hook and a scale just outside the office, so I heaved my pack onto the hook. I was hoping for about 35

pounds, but checked in at 42 pounds. When I looked at the three other entries on the page of the register, I noticed, with some relief, that mine was the second lightest load of the four. In those early days, I saw many people who appeared to be lugging around at least a junior refrigerator, so my burden, while heavy, didn't strike me as being too out of line. However, pack weight assumed more importance as time wore on.

We then returned to the lodge, grateful to be missing several hundred steps up from the office. Behind the lodge, we found the entrance to the Springer Mountain Approach Trail. This was it, the moment that we had been putting off all morning. And, when the moment arrived, it had the power to feel as if time had stopped.

A couple of pictures, with brave smiles, then I was holding on to Diane as if my life depended upon it. I wanted to move but I didn't want to let her go. Eventually, we untangled from one another and I set off, the tears falling freely as I took those first steps. I waved once, then disappeared into the trees.

Not surprisingly, my training in Florida, a state with a total elevation gain of about 40 feet, made me completely unprepared for that initial uphill. I was soon leaking liberally from every orifice, as the sweat overtook my tears and I became spectacularly soaked. This was a condition to which I would grow further accustomed in the coming months. My first hiking lesson was also learned, in that what goes up must come down. That opening assault upon my senses—as I lurched up the first incline—was followed by a flat path that allowed me to recover my gasping breath, before the path headed down. All novice hikers quickly learned that the only reason a path went down in front of you was to enable it to present you with a steep climb in the not-too-distant future.

The narrowness of the path also struck me as incongruous for such an iconic trail. I even imagined that it would get wider once we got onto the real thing, as opposed to the approach trail. However, at very few parts of the Appalachian Trail is the path more than about one to two feet wide. On this early spring morning, the discarded leaves of the deep winter were strewn around, often crunching underfoot.

I had imagined that there would be a steady climb upwards for about seven miles, though the evidence of my eyes, lungs, and legs suggested otherwise. After about an hour, it seemed that I had spent as much time descending as I had ascending, leaving me with the conclusion that the entire climb was still to come. As with pretty much every assumption I made in those early weeks, I was completely wrong. After about four hours of lurching, gasping, and cursing, I emerged at the top of Springer Mountain at the southern terminus of the Appalachian Trail.

To be honest, I was pleased with myself because I hadn't quit on the approach trail, which I understand somebody did that very morning. I would have been mortified if I'd thrown in the towel with minus miles as my A.T. total.

My plan had been to reach the Springer Mountain Shelter before dark, then set up camp there overnight. Without any idea of how long it was going to take to finish the approach trail, I had set myself this modest target. Having done all the uphill stuff, I felt it was time to take stock. It was still early, probably no later than 2 o'clock, so, with plenty of time to kill, I took in my surroundings.

There is a gap through the trees at the top of the mountain and I was able to get a good preview of how I'd be feeling over the coming weeks. I looked with a mixture of awe and disbelief as I took in the scene, along with several other hikers. We considered not only how much we had done on this day but also how much we had to do in the coming months. The sun was bright, even though it was fairly chilly, but I was warm and felt very excited by the prospect of more scenes like this. The opening through the bare trees allowed us to see mountains stretching into the distance. The sight of apparently endless mountains and valleys over the next six months played out everywhere we went. Towns appeared to have been removed from our consciousness. Having been a city dweller for the vast majority of my life, this extrication from an urban lifestyle was liberating. I couldn't hear a car, or see a building. As a novice hiker, this was especially thrilling for me. I'm not too sure what I expected to see, yet the view was something that never, ever, grew old.

I was standing by the southern terminus sign, a bronze plaque that validates your climb. It is also a gateway to the rest of the trip, so I got several pictures of myself sitting by it. Having filled my memory bank with the view from the top, then signed the trail log to record my intention, I turned to move on. I was about to take my first step on the trail and I was feeling the momentous nature of that very first step when I walked straight into an overhanging branch. For a second or two I was stunned, and all sorts of thoughts—none of them good— rushed into my head. As, indeed, did a bump the size of a small egg, which lodged itself prominently about three inches above my right eye. The bump looked even worse since it was also completely unprotected by hair.

I was more embarrassed than hurt and, after solicitous inquiries from my fellow travelers, took my second, third, and fourth steps without further incident, then continued on my less than merry way.

I'm not sure if it was the bang on the head, my excitement, or simply my inability to correctly judge about 350 yards, but I blew past the entrance to the Springer Mountain Shelter and carried on down the mountain. Missing a turn on the A.T. isn't as dumb as it may seem. Hikers need to be constantly looking at their feet in order to prevent a catastrophic fall through impact with rocks or roots. That was particularly so in these early stages. I went so far past this turn that by the time I realized that I must have missed the blue blaze that leads to the shelter, I had about a 15-minute return journey.

This was not a good start. When you have nearly 2,200 miles to walk, banging your head and missing a turn within a quarter of a mile does not augur well for the remainder of your trip. In my optimistic way, however, I chose to look on the bright side: I had reached the top of Springer and I wasn't dead. Walking into camp, I felt that it had been a relatively good day.

I wish that I had been more aware of my first night's companions on that Saturday evening, since there were quite a few people in and around the Springer Mountain Shelter. However, somebody I can recall meeting, and who I ran into later on my journey, was a young woman named Hawkeye. She was with her father and a college friend. The other two were only hiking for a short period, perhaps one or two weeks, while Hawkeye intended to go all the way to Maine. She was a very assured hiker and struck me immediately as someone who would follow through on her ambition. Mind you, coming from a novice such as me, that isn't that great a recommendation. I was delighted when I saw her along the way, especially when I ran into her near the end, in Maine.

Now that my tent was securely on the ground, albeit at a somewhat jaunty angle, I actually found my new home to be considerably more snug than I had imagined. With my pack sitting like an uninvited guest at the foot of my sleeping quilt, to the left, there was still plenty of room for my feet and the other accoutrements of nightly life.

This was an early indication that, really, we don't need too much stuff in our life, and I had all I needed to be cozy. My quilt was beautifully warm, made warmer still by a silk liner, while the air pad made for a soft, comfortable base. There was a headlamp right next to me, should I need to get out of the tent during the night. I had also treated myself by bringing my iPad, so I was able to read from my Kindle app. Indeed, I was doing this when I completely crashed. The exhaustion of the day, both emotional and physical, finally got to me and I fell deeply asleep. However, with my air pad constantly shifting in the tent, it wasn't long before I woke once more.

Suddenly alert, I was alone, in the dark and in the woods. Despite my lack of experience, I didn't feel the least bit concerned, listening intently as I absorbed the deep quiet of the woods. My tent was about 30 yards from the shelter, and the intense silence suggested that everybody had their snoring in check. I could hear absolutely nothing other than gently moving branches. The winter had still not lost its grip on the forest, so rustling leaves above our heads were still several weeks ahead of us.

I tried to get back to sleep as the night wore on and doubtless nodded off from time to time. The dawn came and I felt unrested but happy that my first night was in my rear mirror and I was about to set out on my hike.

Chapter 5: Early Days

When I started to consider the logistics of my hike, I decided to follow advice I'd read from many quarters: for the first few weeks I should restrict my hiking to only about seven or eight miles a day and rarely stretch myself past ten miles. All the while I'd be doing this, I was expecting to be taking witty and pithy little videos, as well as loads of pictures that I'd post online. Each night I'd be updating my blog with stylish, thrilling stories of the day, with just the right balance between journaling and commentary.

I'm sure that it will surprise nobody that none of this happened and my entire plan went to rat shit within the first 20 miles. I'll return to that in a moment as, while we're on the subject of rat shit, I need to take a quick diversion.

Another of my early concerns on this trip, and I'll put it no higher than a concern, was the fact that I would need to have a complete reappraisal of my toiletry habits. I'm something of a man of routine, so changing my normal 15-minute morning session of reading on the throne was always going to be tricky for me. Of immediate concern during that first night was an absolute certainty that the day would break and I would need to avail myself of the facilities. Even worse, I wondered if it would happen in pitch darkness. I had scouted around the shelter to find the route to the nearest water source when I first got there. Finding the route to the privy was of secondary, though only marginally so, importance. Once I had my bearings, I was comfortable that, should my need become urgent in the night, I'd be able to find it again.

Like clockwork, and well before first light, I got the calling. With more confidence than I was feeling, I pulled on my shorts, a fleece and my camp shoes, switched on my headlamp and unzipped my tent. Nothing moved. The air was cold, though still, and I found the blue-blazed trail to the camp privy. The value of my headlamp became immediately apparent as, without it, I would have barely been able to see a hand in front of my face. Conversely, of course, had the lamp revealed a couple of staring eyes just off the trail, I might have needed to reach the privy a little sooner.

Privies are probably the main reason old guys like to camp at shelters. The alternative, which I'll discuss later, is spectacularly unappealing and would never become a comfortable circumstance for me.

I found the privy, which was an unattractive wooden structure, elevated for obvious reasons. The primitive building contained a toilet—normally with a seat—and a bucket of wood chips. The idea was that you do what you came there for, then throw in a bunch of wood chips from the bucket to facilitate the breakdown of your recent deposit. Apparently, this was also helpful in cutting down the inevitable smell, yet I can attest with absolute certainty that the second part of this wasn't working in the least. Those with delicate stomachs may well reconsider if the trail is for them, as this process never improved over the whole 2,200 miles of the Appalachian Trail.

I went about my business, cutting my normal 15 minutes to about two, lobbed in a few wood chips in the general direction of my recent efforts, and stumbled back into the darkness.

Sorry for that detour, but I needed to get it out of my system, so to speak.

As I was saying, my plans were to fully document my hike with blogs, videos, and photos. I was excited by the prospect of doing all this, since my adventure was taking place in an era of rapidly expanding digital coverage and possibilities. Hikers could use phones and tablets to record everything. It amazed me that I was able to take a picture, even at the top of a mountain, and instantly upload it to my blog or Facebook page. Friends and family could share my moment almost as soon as I had experienced it. Also, I'd be able to call my wife to let her know where I was every night. Being married to a woman of Puerto Rican heritage has its delights, though calmness in the face of potential danger to her husband isn't one of them. I knew she wouldn't sleep if she didn't hear from me, so the last call of the day was normally made from high ground, a mile or so short of my shelter for the night.

While some people may frown at this new technological development—and I totally respect that view—I embrace it. Despite looking forward to a sizable chunk of wilderness, balancing that through contact with the outside world was still important to me.

All this wonderful techy stuff was going to happen because I had been given a solar charger by Diane for Christmas. However, I didn't consider for one moment that exposure to sunlight was something of a prerequisite to its success. The charger was attached to my pack, at the top, but appeared incapable in the early days of gaining sufficient charge to power more than about five minutes on my phone. This was bitterly disappointing, yet, until I was able to get to a hostel, there wasn't much I could do about it. The only real benefit with my charger was that, in hostels or motels, I could charge it in the normal way, then use it to recharge my phone when the phone died later on the trail. Writing my blog in town, using scant notes I would take on my iPad, was a compromise I had to make.

In those early days, I was trying to find a rhythm to my hike, so starting with a solid breakfast soon became important to me. While some hikers steered clear of a cooking system to save weight, I was adamant that I needed some heat in my food to sustain me. I couldn't imagine starting the day without a cup of coffee, albeit instant coffee.

So, as I had the night before when preparing my dinner, I joined a couple of the other hikers at the picnic table in front of the shelter. I spread myself out, with my food bag, Jetboil Flash, cup, bowl, and water bottle competing for space.

While my diet changed over the course of the hike, I always had oatmeal in some form or other for breakfast. At this early stage, I just poured a couple of packs of oatmeal into my plastic bowl and stirred in boiling water with my spork. I wasn't as adventurous as some, who thought nothing of adding peanut butter or even olive oil as a piquant addition to the oatmeal. Olive oil was regarded as an efficient way to carry, and thus consume, 100 calories very easily. Calorific accumulation would assume greater importance for me later in the hike.

We all sat around chatting, any barriers instantly dissolved, with friendships, however temporary, forming instantly. The main topic was where we were all heading for the day. For me, that was easy. Hawk Mountain Shelter was just under eight miles away and, with my plan in mind, that was the only realistic place for me to stay the night. Gooch Mountain Shelter, at more than 15 miles, was too far and, toilet arrangements notwithstanding, camping away from a shelter wasn't even on my radar in those first few days.

Now that the first night was under my belt, my toiletry duties had been discharged, and my breakfast was sloshing around inside me, there was nothing for it but to get on my way.

Repacking everything was a daily chore, though, as with most things in life, it got easier with time and familiarity. My novice status showed through on this and many other mornings because, even though I was one of the first to get out of bed, I was one of the last to leave camp. I took well over 1,000 miles before I could be on my way within an hour of getting out of bed. Even then, it was always a close-run thing.

Hiking alone quickly became comfortable to me, though I often envied the easy friendships of others in that first week. Mind you, I also soon discovered that if I saw three people hiking together, then only the one in the lead was going at the right speed. That person would set the pace and the followers were compromising in order to stay together. I found that I had great difficulty hiking with anybody else, so going solo was better for me. Even when I teamed up later on the hike, we would all choose our own pace, often a couple of hundred yards apart.

Another thing that I learned on that first morning, and something that continued to delight me for weeks, was the amazing adaptability of the human body. Hiking is all about ups, downs, and flats. The struggles uphill, particularly in the early days, were the most daunting for me. Not only did my legs cry out in pain, but my lungs also took their turn in letting me know that this wasn't working for them either. I would have to stop every 30 or 40 yards to either gasp for breath or rest my legs, usually both. This continued for probably the first 200 miles.

Coming to the crest of a hill, a wonderful thing would happen. The muscles that had carried me uphill—mainly the quads and glutes—would automatically disengage, having bombarded me with lactic acid to the point of physical pain. Other muscles would kick in to help take the load, with the calves and hamstrings putting in their bit. It was a constantly altering feature of walking dependent purely upon the angle at which I walked. When you've got the forest to yourself, you notice these things.

I made it to Hawk Mountain Shelter in about six hours, having given myself a good break of 30 minutes for lunch. My pace was not fast enough or, at least, not fast enough if I wanted to get to the end before Christmas. Realistically, I had figured, getting to Katahdin should take me about six months. I was very keen to be finished and home in time for Diane's birthday on September 27. Despite my first day's efforts, I rationalized that I would improve as my legs strengthened, I lost some weight, and my lungs improved their capacity. I thought I hadn't done too badly with my legs, although the lung function was scary in those early days. The lactic acid would come, but I knew it would dissipate, so I just had to wait. However, the breathing was difficult in that first week and I had real doubts that it would improve. Happily, I was wrong.

At Hawk Mountain Shelter I met up with many of my first-night friends and found a few more. We all quickly slipped into the routine of the night before and the whole process repeated itself.

Short-term relationships build up over the trip, though I didn't expect to see much more of the family of four that I met that night. The family was made up by mother and father, with their ten- and 15-year-old daughters. They were home-schooling the kids en route, and deserved much credit for giving their girls such an adventure. However, when I came upon the father a few days later, about 300 yards in front of his family, his tension was clear. I asked him how his ten-year-old was coping. He replied, more than a little tersely I thought, that a better question would be how he was coping. I told him that would have been my question had I known him better. He grunted and told me that he'd better head back and help his family. As he passed me, he muttered that perhaps he needed to get more patience. I never saw them again, and reflected at the time how brave they had been to try this as a group. I had enough on my plate keeping myself safe; I couldn't imagine having responsibility for another soul, and certainly not young kids.

Retiring again at "hiker midnight," which I was led to believe is the time that the sun disappears, I settled down for a second night in my tent. I had once more totally failed to realize the need to find a flat spot, so sleep was elusive as I ran over the events of the day.

I had started at just over 3,500 feet and had walked downhill to 2,500 feet for about four miles. Of course, having learned the what-goes-up-must-come-down lesson, the next three miles took me back up to nearly 3,500 feet before descending slightly to Hawk Mountain Shelter.

The guidebook had warned me that Army Rangers from a nearby military camp used the area for training exercises. Apparently, they had been spotted at "all times of the day and night." I was grateful that I had neither seen nor heard the Rangers during the day, so peaceful had my hike been. The night provided them with new opportunities, and they decided that pissing off a bunch of smelly hikers would be a lot of fun. Consequently, they spent the vast majority of the night zooming along just above the trees in their Ospreys, hovering directly over us. In a house, that may not have been too noisy, but in a tent it sounded like the Third World War.

The following morning, one of my new friends, Grizzly Bear from Maine, told us over breakfast that he had hiked the trail 15 years before and stayed at this shelter. Rangers had clearly chosen to up their game and had been rope-lined directly into the camp. I recall thinking that had this happened the previous night, my trip to the privy would have been moved up the agenda by a few hours.

Grizzly Bear from Maine had decided that, my own choice of name notwithstanding, he was going to call me "England,"—precisely what I was trying to avoid. He was the same age as me, though, with his straggly, gray beard, he looked several years older. He also bore more than a passing resemblance to Santa Claus, an effect that he was clearly aware of, for he produced a Santa hat a few days later to general amusement. Grizz eventually dropped off the pace a little, and I learned later from several other hikers that he caught Lyme disease, bringing his hike to an end somewhere near New York. He was a terrific character and an imposing presence on the trail.

We were all finding our feet at this stage, and nothing bonds a group more than sitting round a campfire at night. Fortunately, there were volunteers for this practice, so I spent several happy hours staring into the fire. I would warm one side of my face or the other as my more energetic, younger friends scattered around finding logs and twigs to burn.

While all hikers greeted each other on equal terms, the older people, especially in the early days, gravitated to one another, and the youngsters tended to do likewise. Still trying to establish my hiking bona fides, people like Grizz and a few other of the older guys allowed me to ease myself into the hike. I spent much of the first three days around them, mostly because they were as slow as I was.

There was one Korean-American guy, Bill, who had made a spiritual commitment to hike the trail. He believed that God had chosen this as a task for him, and Bill had answered. Unfortunately, God hadn't warned him that carrying a 60-lb pack, in light of his pre-diabetic condition and copious medications, wasn't a smart move. I passed Bill at about 3 o'clock on my way to Gooch Mountain Shelter, where I arrived about an hour later.

It was a fancier shelter than most, with two sleeping levels and an extended roofline to allow cover above the picnic table. Hikers approached it via a long, curving path around the mountain, with the shelter permanently in sight—across a deep valley—for about 20 minutes. Arriving there and settling down, everybody was entertained when a couple of the hardier youngsters dived off the path, hurtled down the mountain, and scrambled up to the shelter, cutting off about 400 yards of trail.

The discussion turned to Bill and we wondered where he was. I remarked that I had passed him about an hour earlier, and that he had been struggling under his huge pack. Immediately, two of the youngsters, led by Hawkeye, rounded up a posse of seven or eight, who set off without their packs to find Bill. The oldies agreed that this was a different breed of kids from the type we were normally exposed to. We soon became the stereotypical old farts sitting around and moaning about "kids today." I shudder as I recall how judgmental I was.

A triumphant procession arrived about 45 minutes after they had left, each hiker carrying part of Bill's pack. He was led, still puffing and panting, into camp. He quit the trail the following morning, realizing that he wasn't up to it. He rationalized his decision by declaring that God had other plans for him. Bill felt that his God had made him do these few days on the A.T. to show him the good in people. I guess some folks can find reinforcement in their beliefs in everything.

Chapter 6: Our first stop

I had planned with Diane that my first stop back in civilization would happen when I reached Woody Gap. This gap was about 21 miles into the hike, hopefully on day four. I would be able to get a shuttle into Suches, pick up my package from the post office, shower, launder, charge my phone, eat relentlessly, then sleep in a bed. While I hadn't developed the legendary hiker hunger by this stage, eating relentlessly appealed to me greatly. Doing some laundry and taking a shower wouldn't go amiss either.

In the way of information transmission on the trail, several others were also intending to stop at Woody Gap. By the time about six of us had gathered on the road, we called the shuttle. My memory is a little hazy as to who my fellow occupants in the back of the truck were that day, though I know for sure that two of them were a pair of German girls, each with a dog. My reason for remembering this is that one of the dogs took a liking to me, nuzzled up, then unleashed a fart that could only have come from some doggy depths beyond human experience. God knows what the poor thing had been eating, but I couldn't imagine it was anything too wholesome. The girls thought it was hilarious and the dog, eying me suspiciously, just sat there looking at me as if I'd been the one who'd farted. Amazingly, I started to feel guilty.

Quite why people think that bringing their pet on the trail would enhance their experience, I can't imagine. All the hikers I met who had dogs with them swore that their dog was loving every minute of it. However, seeing the poor things in the morning getting their packs fitted onto their backs often told a different story. Most of them looked so miserable that they adopted a kind of sideways, shuffling stance. Looking miserable is a tough thing for a dog to achieve, by the way. I imagined to myself that a dog, after a day of 15 or so miles, would get into camp and say, in doggy lingo, "Thank God that's over," only to be fitted again the following morning with its pack. "We're going again?" This would continue for six months and the poor thing would have no idea that it wasn't a Sisyphean task that he was doomed to repeat for eternity.

My opinion of dogs on the trail took a further, more dramatic turn about two months later, but I'll come to that in good time. Suffice it to say, I never came around to the idea that having pets on the trail was a good idea.

While we had been waiting for the shuttle, I spoke with a young guy, Sam. He was ex-military, and we hit it off immediately. I approached him because he was shivering; his lips were actually turning blue. It wasn't that it was so cold that day, though it was probably in the low 40s. Rather, his water container had exploded in his bag and had soaked all his clothes, including those he was wearing. He had nothing dry to put on and hadn't arranged to stay in Suches. He looked in bad shape. I suggested that there was bound to be plenty of room at the hostel, and that he should join us. He scrambled gratefully up onto the truck bed.

I wasn't sure what to expect from Suches and other similar towns on the trail, but they were mostly linked by a lack of anything to do and one central hub for hikers to gather. The hostel was part of the Wolf Pen Gap Country Store. While it was a substantial building, that was just about all there was to see. There was a post office next door, but the store dominated what I saw of Suches, with ice and gas available outside, and food, laundry, and TV inside.

The hostel was upstairs and was obviously a new experience for me, with co-ed apparently the norm. Once everybody had unloaded, we all worked on our priorities. For all of us, the first thing we did was establish where to charge our phones and get connected to Wi-Fi, then check our emails. I'd thought that I was the oddity by wanting to stay in touch with home, but I was pleased to see that it was uniformly important to my fellow travelers.

The single dorm had about 15 bunk beds, made from a wooden frame with a piece of plywood as a sort of box spring. I knew we weren't in the Ritz, but I'd hoped for a mattress. Instead, my pad and quilt came out once more.

The more experienced hikers had worked out that laundry facilities were in short supply and had nabbed the two machines. By the time I caught on to this, I was well down the line. However, given that there was not much to do other than eat pizza and watch TV, I set up by the laundry room to keep my spot. After 21 miles of hiking, this was a change, and I was thoroughly content to pay scant attention to the TV while writing my blog. From that day forward I was always very aware of the need to resolve housekeeping issues in the first couple of minutes after arriving anywhere.

Another first was the dilapidated shower room and the sharing of soap that seemed to be part of the hiker's routine. When you haven't showered for four days and have built up layer upon layer of sweat and grime, the niceties of everyday life soon dissolve into the distant past. The warmth of the water on my body and the squeaky-clean feeling that I got from the shower made this one of my finest bathroom experiences ever. With my bald head, I didn't need even need to share hair products. As a consequence, by the time I settled down for the night, I felt calm, clean, fed, and watered. There were freshly washed clothes in my pack, along with the new supply of food that Diane had mailed me.

Of course, my 60-year-old bladder required a nighttime wander, and I managed to tread on both of the dogs as I plotted a path to the bathroom, waking most of the dorm along the way. I'm afraid an aging bladder will do that to you.

That night in my bunk, I had time to reflect upon the first few days of my adventure, rightly realizing that this was the way it was going to be for the foreseeable future. Preconceived notions had already deserted me and I was rapidly becoming accustomed to a kind of feral living that would only develop in the coming months.

Grizzly Bear from Maine was with us that evening, and he had given me good advice on how to look at the composition of a thru-hike. He pointed out that it was easier to regard the Appalachian Trail as a series of adventures, interspersed with stops in towns to refresh and revive. In that way, I could look at the first four days as one such adventure. I had hiked, I was now resting, and looking forward to my next adventure. I really like context and this gave it to me. I listened contentedly to my fellow adventurers breathe, snore, whisper, fart, and laugh. This was going to be my life for the next six months. I realized that I could do it.

Lying there in the dark, I reminded myself that one of my unexpressed fears before the trip had been whether or not I'd be able to go several days at a time without a drink. To most people, that may seem ridiculous, but I come from a family with, at best, urges and, at worst, addictions. I referred earlier to the fact that I drank a little more than was strictly necessary. While that was true, it was a wild understatement. I once remarked to a group of American friends that things were very different in the U.S. with regard to the drinking culture. This was notably so when compared with England. I said, more as a throwaway remark than anything else that, for the previous 30 or so years, I had woken every morning, seven days a week and 52 weeks of the year, with a hangover. My statement may have been a touch hyperbolic, but not far away from the absolute truth. The plain fact is that I thought everybody did that. I would think nothing of drinking three or four bottles of wine and several glasses of vodka in a day. I didn't even regard drinking a few beers as drinking.

The insurance industry, especially my branch of it, the reinsurance industry, wallowed in such a lifestyle, with lunches often taking four or more hours. Expense accounts were used to fuel my lifestyle, and I participated more enthusiastically than most. In retrospect, I thought, as I lay in the hostel that night, meeting Diane had modified my behavior. Since meeting her, my limit has been two or three glasses of wine, though I still drink something every day. In fact, I smile every time I replace the cork in a bottle; in my past, I had never, ever, done such a thing. If a bottle of wine was open, it would be finished, whether or not I had company. There was even a part of me that preferred not to have company so as to enjoy an entire bottle, or bottles, by myself.

I'd just hiked for four days and hadn't touched a drop of booze. As I drifted off to sleep, I recognized that I'd already been able to make a fundamental change in my life. It may not be much to people who don't drink to excess, and I certainly don't intend to convince anybody that it is the case, but three or four days without a drink to somebody like me is fundamental. If you don't get it, feel free to move on. If you do, then you'll understand how pleased I was with my progress.

Chapter 7: Neels Gap

Getting back to Woody Gap the following day, my fellow hikers and I were reminded how exposed we were to disaster. Two young women from New Hampshire must have reached the gap after us. They had hoped to go into Suches but, with dead cell phones, were unable to call the shuttle. The temperatures were falling precipitously, and they faced the prospect of a dangerously cold night without shelter. There was a makeshift public bathroom at the Gap, providing minimal cover, but they had no alternative. One of these women was Bluebird, who was thru-hiking all the way to Maine, while her friend was just doing the first couple of weeks. They spent the night shivering on the bathroom floor, grateful to get moving the following morning. Their plight was a reminder to us all that danger was always potentially around the corner, even for those who had planned ahead.

This was my longest day of hiking so far, brought about more by circumstance than design. I was heading up and over Blood Mountain, the highest point on the trail in Georgia, and had hoped to stay in the shelter at the top. However, I had learned at Suches that there were reports of aggressive bears in this area and that a new requirement had been imposed by whoever the authorities were. Bear canisters were now the rule for protecting food supplies and so, since I didn't possess one of these, I had to walk further than usual, on to Neels Gap.

Blood Mountain was a steady climb of about five miles,

gaining 1,500 feet, after an initial up and over Big Cedar Mountain first thing in the morning. With my muscles engaging and disengaging at the appropriate times, I enjoyed this trek as a test of my improving strength on the trail. At the top, as always, I was greeted by views that never failed to impress. I started scrambling around on the rocks to establish a good spot for a video and a couple of photographs. It was very liberating, with the difficulties of the climb behind me. A bunch of us took in the sun on another cold day. With new friends sharing the scene and taking pictures of one another, the whole thing felt very collegiate.

I had brought a gizmo with me called a StickPic, which fixed on the end of my hiking pole and attached to my phone. This little beauty let me take long-distance selfies, allowing me the effect of having somebody filming me on my hike. I was sitting on a rock, having just recorded a panoramic view of everything below us on Blood Mountain. I was removing the StickPic from my pole when my phone, which I had balanced on my thigh, fell off. I knew before I even looked that this wasn't going to be good, so loudly had the phone cracked on impact with the ground. With a heavy heart, I reached down and saw the inevitably cracked screen. I was crushed. I was on day five of about 180 days; the chances of getting to the end with a phone that worked were remote.

In "real life," I suppose I would have rushed to AT&T, signed up for a new phone, and moved on. At the top of Blood Mountain, miles from anywhere, I quickly came to terms with the new state of my phone and was forced to move on. My options were, by circumstance, limited. I hadn't taken long to learn that there was no alternative, so I simply got on with my hike. Having few options tends to push one towards acceptance far quicker in the woods than it does in so-called normal circumstances. I learned throughout the hike that fewer options made for happier, easier decisions, and it was pointless sweating over stuff you couldn't do anything about.

With the highlight of Blood Mountain now over, there was a reasonably steep descent of about two miles into Neels Gap and my second consecutive night in a hostel. While it hadn't been in my plan, I wasn't unhappy with this development. However, the stop showed me the wide variety of accommodations that can be experienced when not in the woods.

Neels Gap is one of those stops that has attracted a kind of A.T. folklore, with the shakedown of hikers' packs to the forefront. This takes place in the outfitter's shop at Neels Gap and is a reassessment of exactly what a hiker is carrying and what he or she should be carrying. From my observation, the word "shakedown" was something of a *double entendre*, with the shop advising the purchase of new bags, tents, even backpacks. Dispensing with weight is clearly an expensive business, as I saw a number of people leaving the shop considerably lighter, if only in their wallet.

I had found my stay in Suches the previous evening to be an enjoyable experience, so that was the yardstick by which I'd judge this night's accommodation. However, I soon discovered that hostel could just as easily be spelled "hostile." This place—which shared the building with the outfitter—was dreadful, by far the worst I experienced on my trip. To be fair, I was offered two options. The first was to stay in the hostel, while the second was to share a cabin with three other hikers.

The cost of these options would work out pretty much the same and, neither for the first nor the last time, I chose badly. Staying in a cabin would involve a walk downhill and I wanted to avoid any more exercise for the day.

The previous evening, I had been warm, cozy even, with all amenities within yards. The dump that I was in could not have offered a sharper contrast, for it was cold, dark, and generally nasty. Most of the hikers who chose to stay there had to put clothes on as they entered, not take them off—it was freezing. So much so that I went outside with a couple of guys, and we found it warmer there than inside.

There was a kitchen with no hot water and, when the owner came in, I asked him if he could get some more heat into the place. We were talking in the dorm room and he carelessly pointed behind him, without looking, to the heater on the wall in the sitting room, telling me that it would meet our needs. Well, he actually pointed at the wall where the heater had once been, for it was nowhere to be seen. There was a fireguard in front of the space, but no actual heater. We both looked wordlessly at this spot, as if a heater would miraculously materialize. We even gave it a few seconds on the off-chance that the miracle would occur. Not surprisingly, we were disappointed. Seeing that he had my attention as well as my disappointment, he went for broke by telling me that the restroom was also out of use. So, I would have a 2 a.m. walk if my bladder was going to behave as normal. This was something to look forward to, given the need to walk outside in the cold to a public restroom about 50 yards away. The man didn't think to apologize. Not for the only time on this trip, I was made aware that hikers are something of an inconvenience to be tolerated, as opposed to being a constituency to be treated as customers. I should also point out that the showers and laundry were within the public restroom, to compound the unpleasantness of my stay.

Mind you, to say something nice about the place, they did have a great selection of videos, and I was reintroduced to the magic that is *Blazing Saddles*. I was watching it in my full cold-weather gear, with my hood cinched tightly to keep the cold from penetrating. You may be thinking that I was alone in this criticism, but you'd be wrong. Everybody who had stayed in Suches the previous evening was just as appalled by the contrast, though most were less vociferous about it than I was. My wife refers to it as getting very British about things. While she loves me dearly, it is rarely a compliment.

The following morning, having endured the cold of the night, I couldn't wait to get away from this hell hole. After a quick coffee and oatmeal, I left it behind. The previous day had been a ten-mile hike and the one to come was going to be just over 11 miles, so I felt that I was stepping up my efforts and making steady progress.

There was now a coterie of hikers with whom I was bonding, and I spent the day drifting between them as we all made various rest and food stops. Coming upon a fellow traveler normally entailed a quick chat, a shared meal, or just a casual greeting. It was never awkward, and always heartwarming, to feel part of a traveling band, albeit one that constantly formed then reformed.

I was heading for Low Gap Shelter, and this day was my first to experience the truly delightful concept of Trail Magic. I'd heard that this was an unexpected kindness that hikers would receive on the trail. To be frank, I hadn't expected too much. Again, I was spectacularly wrong, and it is difficult to describe just how Trail Magic, in its many forms, can impact your day while hiking. On this day, I was alone and about two miles short of Tesnatee Gap when I met a fellow hiker coming the other way. He was a section hiker, and was backtracking to rejoin his partner, who had fallen behind. He told me that I would run into this phenomenon in a couple of miles and he believed that there were burgers to be had. For me, this was wonderful news, because burgers were regarded as one of the ultimate Trail Magic treats. I hurried on, telling fellow hikers as they passed me or I passed them.

My friend appeared to have overstated the case for this Trail Magic session, for it turned out that Cheez-Its and donuts were the *cuisine du jour*, while burgers were nowhere to be seen. Despite this slight disappointment, I filled my face with as much junk food and as many calories as I could reasonably justify. Given my voracious intake, it would have been a touch impolite to have asked after the burgers. However, the point of Trail Magic was that it was always a wonderful thing to find, and all hikers were delighted to discover it. The group at Tesnatee Gap was affiliated with a church and Trail Magic was the members' way of helping hikers on their difficult journey. We sat, ate, and chatted about the hike; not once did anybody try to impose his or her religious views on me. They were good people doing good things for fellow travelers. If that isn't a Christian attitude, I don't know what is.

Trail Magic was so prevalent in the early stages of the hike that there came a time when, approaching a road, I would put off a snack in order to see if there was some magic to be had. That may sound a trifle calculating, but my delight wasn't in saving money; it was more to revel in the kindness of others. I was always incredibly grateful for the efforts expended on my, and my fellow travelers', behalf.

Chapter 8: Time to think

Before I left home for the hike, I had received a couple of warnings from friends, some of whom claimed to know a thing or two about hiking. The one that stuck with me was from an old school pal who was then living in Barcelona. He and a friend had walked El Camino, a Spanish pilgrimage that doubles as a hike, a few years before, and they had written a book about their journey.

His comment to me concerned the loneliness that is inevitably part of the experience, referring to it as "like meditation, only with blisters." He noted that we are all surrounded in our normal lives by distractions, like TV,

Facebook, and iPads. He went on to say that without those distractions, your thoughts can overwhelm you. Interestingly, he also commented that this loneliness was both the worst and the best part of the trip.

As it happened, I thoroughly enjoyed the silence of the woods in the first 800 miles of my hike, for silence there was. I'd expected a cacophony of birdsong, but was taken aback by how little of it I heard. I had my phone and my music with me, along with headphones, yet not once in those 800 miles did I listen to anything other than the noises, or lack of them, around me while walking. I took the delicious opportunity to think through the many moral dilemmas that exist in our lives and pretty much resolved most of those, to my satisfaction, in my head.

A liberal by nature—and I noticed a preponderance of liberals on the trail—I tried to work through what I thought about war, about poverty, about race, and, this being America, what I thought about guns and abortion. Once that philosophical task was complete, I turned to the life I've led and the people to whom I have caused pain. This was a disgracefully long list and far too long, and private, to fully record here. However, there are a number of people I have wronged who deserve a public apology, even if they may not want to hear it.

Having confessed to an insatiable desire for booze for the majority of my life, I suppose that confessing to a similar attitude to women wouldn't be too much of a stretch.

When I was only 22, I married my first real girlfriend, Pearl. She was beautiful, intelligent, and put up with more of my excesses than she probably should have, yet we remained married for 12 years. I was unfaithful from the start, having regular and dangerous affairs that completely disregarded the vows I had made. I've thought a lot about what it is to be unfaithful and have come to the conclusion—this was before the trail, by the way—that once you are unfaithful, then you will always be an unfaithful person. You may never cross the line again, you may well live an exemplary life, but the way you are able to casually cross that line in the first place absolutely defines you as such. It is a bit like Caesar crossing the Rubicon, committing himself to a path from which there was no return. In my view, this has nothing to do with forgiveness or even redemption; it is simply a transition from being one thing to being another.

Staying faithful to the person I love has been a constant concern for me, though age has moderated my behavior as a direct correlation to my reducing booze intake, accompanied, no doubt, by a reduced attractiveness to women. I believe that being aware of my foibles in this regard is critical to managing my life and, most importantly, my marriage. Self-awareness has come at a price, both financial and emotional, and has taken me a long time to learn.

I spent several hours on the trail apologizing to Pearl, so heinous were my transgressions.

My second wife was Diane. Yes, in a life of three marriages, fate decided to nudge me in the ribs by giving me two women named Diane to marry. By a somewhat strange quirk of fate, my second wife's first husband was also a Steve. I left Pearl in 1986, moving in almost immediately with Diane who, almost simultaneously, left her husband. As you would imagine, this was not a coincidence. We had flaunted our relationship openly in the City of London, where I worked, and were even invited to certain social events as a couple for nearly two years. I loved her and didn't care who knew. I will never use booze as an excuse for my behavior, but I will say that it made me so careless as to the consequences of my actions that I often shudder at both those actions and their subsequent consequences.

Diane was just as beautiful, but more harsh than Pearl. We both knew that we had behaved badly and Diane was especially aware of Oscar Wilde's old saying that once you marry your mistress, you create a vacancy. We had a passionate, very intense life together for 15 years, but I started my first affair after only a year of marriage. That affair was with somebody we both knew as a friend and, now that I had the benefit of time to look back at it dispassionately, even I was appalled at my deception.

Ironically, the breaking point for that second marriage was a drunken, careless remark by one of my best friends at a conference in San Francisco. Talk about living by the sword and dying by the sword! I was there with my wife and we were due to fly on to Fiji, in the South Pacific, the following day. We were celebrating our tenth anniversary and, thoughtless infidelities notwithstanding, I was looking forward to the chance to get away with her. That last evening in San Francisco ended, as these things often did, in a bar at our hotel. She was very comfortable on her own, so we split up and played the room, chatting and drinking with clients, friends, and foes alike. A few hours into the drinking session, Diane came up to me and, with a face that had trouble written all over it, asked, "Are we going?" It was something of a rhetorical question, as we clearly were.

In the elevator, on the way up, I tried to speak with her, but she could only manage "In the room," through her anger. We'd had fights before but her rage seemed different and clearly very intense. It turned out that she had been goading my friend and giving him a bit of a hard time over something or other. He must have decided that she needed a taste of her own medicine. He stated, categorically, that I had been having an affair with one of the conference attendees. While this happened to be untrue, it did nothing to mollify Diane when I told her and an immediate barrier came up between us that I could never bring down. I'm sure that the majority of people reading this will feel that it served me right and I entirely agree, even believing that being wrongly accused has a certain poetic justice.

The following morning we left for Fiji, then onto Vatulele, a small, romantic island just off the mainland. The vacation was a disaster, and we returned home at odds with one another. From then on, our marriage was a train wreck in waiting, painfully disintegrating in front of us, without either of us having the ability, or the strength, or possibly the desire, to prevent the inevitable crash. Once more, I had been the instigator and had apparently learned nothing from my awful choices earlier.

We limped on for another 30 or so months, finally calling it a day in July 2001, while I continued to drink and lurch through life in the early 2000s. The breakup of a marriage is rarely taken lightly, even when one or both parties want to get away. It is sad for both, and hurts not only the two involved but also peripheral characters, such as nieces and nephews. There are ripples that don't immediately manifest themselves, yet they are relentless and spread throughout family and friends. I shudder to think about the effect on children.

The apology to Diane wasn't as heartfelt as the one to Pearl, but it took quite a while to get off my chest. There were other apologies, especially to my children, but that is enough for the time being. There are just so much apologies you can make at one time.

And, I talked with God.

I should start by explaining that I come from a fairly secular country and, despite moving to a country which seems to have God enmeshed in its whole being, I have never believed that He exists. You'll see that I still capitalize His name and pronouns, but I guess this is more a defensive measure than anything else. I wanted to try and think through the existence or otherwise of such a being, and, don't worry, I won't bore you with all the reasons I came up with. Suffice to say that, eventually, I decided that I didn't believe. However, I gave it a shot.

Right from the beginning, I made an attempt to speak with Him. Every day, often in the first couple of miles, I would stop, plant my feet firmly on the path, bow my head, and hold my trekking poles together at my waist with my hands touching. Then I'd start talking. I tried to be chatty, introducing myself each morning and asking Him to look after my wife and my kids. I added myself as an afterthought when I started falling with alarming regularity. I also told Him that I was looking for some sort of sign that would allow me to get past my lack of belief. He never answered me nor gave me any indication that I was being heard.

Reading that paragraph back, I know that it all sounds ludicrous, and I have no doubt gone about it entirely the wrong way. Yet it was my way and, really, the way I'd expect to communicate with somebody who apparently volunteered His son to die and save me. I was also aware that I hadn't exactly been as righteous as I might have been, so that may have gone against me. But at this stage in my life, I was a whole lot better person and felt the need to at least try.

Our one-sided conversation went on, every day, for about 1,400 miles. Nothing—though I can't say I was surprised. While you get used to being ignored by your kids, you'd have thought that, if He'd been listening, I might have got a hint. Nada. In the end, having exhausted all possible arguments that I could muster, both for and against, I decided that enough was enough, and I reverted to walking without that quiet moment.

I rather missed it.

Chapter 9: Helen and Hiawassee

It was tricky to drag myself away from Tesnatee Gap. I was made to feel welcome, and people were feeding me. Several other hikers had arrived, and we were treated like superheroes, so iconic has the trail become. But I still had quite a schlep to Low Gap Shelter and the weather was looking unpromising. While rain threatened for the remaining five-and-a-bit miles, it didn't actually start until I arrived, and—thankfully—had put up my tent. I had passed the blue-blazed path down to Whitley Gap Shelter. Stopping at this point would have made it a seven-mile day, but I couldn't bear the thought of a shelter that was about a mile and a quarter from the main trail. When you have about

2,200 miles to hike, an extra couple of miles as a detour is irrationally unwelcome.

It was a wet night and one that reiterated the fact that I hadn't properly embraced the concept of a flat tenting spot. Another epic fail on that score had me sliding around all night again. I also learned that coming into regular contact with the walls of my tent tended to dampen my quilt.

The rain stuck around for most of the night and the following day, demanding that worst of all activities: packing up in the rain. Every morning, I would be specially grateful if I woke without the pitter-patter of raindrops on my tent. To be fair, this was normally the case. At Low Gap Shelter, however, there was little doubt that I was going to be disappointed from the time I woke in the middle of the night, since it was pouring as if Noah was in the vicinity. The rain let up only marginally, so it turned out to be one of those miserable mornings that made hiking so difficult.

My trifecta of awfulness included the following: my pack and its contents were damp, I had to wear wet-weather gear in the knowledge that there would be nothing dry to put on when I got to my destination, and the path became dangerously slippery. Fail, fail, and fail. My biggest problem with wet-weather gear was that I tended to heat up dramatically, then sweat from the inside. Also, after about 30 minutes of heavy rain, my gear lived up to its name by sharing the wetness with me. I'm sure the jacket was designated as waterproof, but I didn't meet anybody who had a jacket that would keep the rain out for more than 30 or 40 minutes. As a consequence, liquid was eventually assaulting me from two directions.

I was hiking with Sam, whom I had bumped into while he was turning blue at Woody Gap. We were heading for an unplanned break at Unicoi Gap. We needed to dry out, so from there we were getting a shuttle into Helen. The town was about nine miles east of the crossing and we had booked a motel. We had a steady climb all day, crossing Blue Mountain at almost exactly 4,000 feet, before descending sharply for just shy of two miles down to under 3,000 feet into Unicoi Gap.

These wet days were equally unrewarding from a vista perspective. However, to complain about this would have been a touch churlish, because we had so far had sun for a good deal of our first 50 miles.

Helen was going to be my first real town, though I soon learned to manage expectations in that regard. The town is actually referred to as a city, in White County, Georgia, on the Chattahoochee River, with a population of just over 500 people. The most remarkable thing about Helen, however, is that it is built as a Bavarian Alps replica town, thankfully without Germans. Having been to the Bavarian Alps in my time, I can confidently report that this is nothing like a German town. The whole place looks like something Disney would have built had Hitler won the Second World War. For my British friends, think the London pub in Disney's Epcot Center and you'll get my drift.

The motel was one of those unattractive, dark-carpeted places with depressing furniture that wouldn't have looked out of place in Hitchcock's *Psycho*—apart from the Indian guy at the front desk. Nonetheless, Sam and I were grateful to hang up our wet stuff and get some laundry done. We then showered and met up with another young guy, Jay (who was eventually named Beans a hundred or so miles later), at Monday's Pub. I made the error of shaving my head in the shower, a process that took about 45 minutes, and cost me about a pint of blood. After that, I vowed to either let my hair grow or get somebody else to shave my head. I looked like I could have auditioned for a zombie movie.

At Monday's, we ordered the biggest burger we could wrap our jaws around, washing it down with several steins of beer. There was an excellent live band and, conversation being more or less impossible, we watched the locals strutting their stuff. And what stuff they had. Monday's was clearly the local meeting place for the unemployable and single. Several 50-year-old women giggled uncontrollably, lasciviously eying the table of Helen's most eligible bachelors across the room.

There were a few unfulfilled rendezvous, but everything paled in comparison to the seven-foot-tall, 60-ish Hell's Angel and the five-foot-tall pelvis-thruster he was with. Her version of dancing was to push pretty much everything below her waistline his way. This was despite the fact that it came into contact around his knee area. Determining that he'd get more bang for his buck, so to speak, he lifted her off her feet. She then wrapped her legs around his waist, gyrating furiously at him once more. Her actions must have awakened the romantic within him. He suddenly prised her away from his pelvic region, with some difficulty it must be said, then put her on the floor, only to drop to one knee, still several inches taller than her, and, apparently, propose. He clearly hadn't planned for this moment of overwhelming romance, as there was no ring to be seen. But, in a moment of inspiration, he gallantly removed his cruddy hat from his head, revealing unkempt, long, gray hair in the process—making him look like Gandalf from *The Lord of the Rings* trilogy—and offered the hat to his lady. I can't tell you the last time I saw something so romantic but so bizarre in equal measure.

Sam and I were late getting back on the road the following morning. This was partly due to the need to ensure everything was as dry as possible, but mainly because we were reluctant to start another day in the rain. Every surface in our room bore an element of our soggy contents, while our tents had spent the night draped over a railing outside. I often left my gear unattended outside bars or shops, even though there were one or two reported incidents of stealing on the trail. There was a general consensus that hikers respected each other's gear, so I never feared losing anything. Consequently, even at this early stage, leaving my tent outside was no big deal. Having delayed the start as long as possible, with an unambitious day of nearly six miles ahead of us, we grabbed a shuttle to take us back to Unicoi Gap.

Tray Mountain was our destination, so we had to trudge, muddily, up and down Rocky Mountain to achieve our modest goal. I found it tough enough to climb 1,000 feet in a mile and a quarter, but exponentially more so when rain added itself to the mix. I was stopping to regain my breath at regular intervals, pushing through the burning pain in my thigh muscles all the while. Peaking, then immediately descending, activated the downhill muscles and the difficulty simply shifted its form, though not its severity.

I was using my poles as carefully as I could, picking my way as if through a muddy minefield. There were a few minor slips every now and then to concentrate the mind, but I managed to keep my footing every time. I was able to gingerly make my way down from Rocky Mountain to a short, flatter stretch before the inevitable climb up Tray Mountain. Relaxing for the first time that day, I then made the first of many spectacular falls while walking along flat ground. One moment I was strolling along, the next I had slipped, pirouetted, and ended up on my fleshy backside in the middle of a bush. This turned out to be a well-positioned bush, preventing me from taking an unscheduled slide about 100 feet down the mountain. Once Sam realized that I hadn't been injured—and that he wouldn't have to alert Search and Rescue—he roared with laughter before helping me unceremoniously to my feet. It was the first of many tumbles and showed me the inherent danger in every step, so I resolved to pay more attention to the supposedly easy parts of the hike. I can report unequivocally that my extra vigilance made no difference whatsoever to my safety.

Following my fall, Sam and I still had another three mile uphill stretch that would take us to nearly 4,500 feet, then down a short way to Tray Mountain Shelter. By now, the wind and rain were whipping around and the severity increased on the way up. We reached the shelter about two hours later, where it was pretty wild. The trees were blowing about violently, with the rain coming at us horizontally. As usual, the shelter was packed and, while everybody was happy to scooch up to let me in, I didn't really fancy it. I found a flat spot to set up for the night.

Returning to the shelter, I had to squeeze in after all, since there was no table at this shelter on which to cook. Some enterprising hiker—in an attempt to mitigate the worst of the wind and rain—had located a tarp at the back of the shelter. He triumphantly made a makeshift cover for the front. Unfortunately, it kept flapping back and forth, so it was a little frantic, and doubtless a fire hazard, as I cooked dinner. Despite our close proximity, everybody was so amenable, moving constantly to make room and making sure that everybody got a chance to feed themselves.

I met a Canadian couple at Tray Mountain Shelter who gave me my first feeling of hiker envy. They had a battery-powered inflator for their air pad and I wanted one. I was already tired of blowing my pad up at the end of the day and this was the perfect answer. For some reason, entirely unaccountable to me even now, I hiked the rest of the trip wanting one of these. However, I never bought one, despite many opportunities in the months to come. I can't explain it, particularly given my penchant for impulse purchases. I guess I was destined to exhaust myself every night in that end-of-the-day, final puff that would complete my tiredness.

With the rain slowly dying down, the wind took up the slack and increased in intensity. The temperature also dropped markedly, so I quickly finished my meal and left the relative safety of the shelter to brave it in my tent. As I said, I had found a flat spot for about the first time, and felt comfortable about the upcoming night. My tent was firmly anchored, nothing was going to roll about, and I had plenty of dry clothing to add to my existing layers. Thinking back to that night, I shudder at my naïveté; I should have squeezed into the shelter. The rain returned, and the temperature plummeted further. I woke at around 3 o'clock, immediately feeling too cold to return to sleep. I pulled on my other pair of socks and put on my fleece, dragging my beanie hat down over my face. I don't mind admitting that I was afraid that I would be unable to stop my own drastically reducing temperature. All of this was so new to me that I had nothing comparable to measure it against, but I was more concerned than I needed to be. At the time, I had no idea if I would stay safe until the morning, and I was very unnerved by this experience. I managed to fall back to sleep; though by the time I awoke, I was still comparatively cold.

It was a Sunday morning. I had decided that I'd have an 11-mile day and treat myself to a room at the Holiday Inn Express in Hiawassee. A hotel was well above my budget, but I wanted to stay in a proper room with unquestionable sheets, an unsullied shower, and a decent TV with a functioning remote control. The night was also going to be my last in Georgia. I was proud of myself in getting this first real milestone under my belt. I still had the 11 miles to negotiate and, wanting to be on my way with Sam, I made a daft error that taught me a lot about my limits on this hike.

Chapter 10: On the way to Hiawassee

I had assumed that the quiet tapping on my tent in the minutes before getting up at Tray Mountain Shelter was rain. I was wrong. The sound turned out to be a light dusting of snow on top of a thin layer of ice. Even looking at my tent that morning made me feel cold, so I was eager to get away. I would normally have my coffee and oatmeal, but I simply wanted to get moving to raise my temperature. While it was cold, it was sunny, and I knew that the walking would soon have me warmed up. Once more, my inexperience won out. I grabbed a quick protein bar, with another one handy to eat about 30 minutes later. In those early days, I was also underestimating how much water I needed, so I failed to replenish that as well.

Your body doesn't lie to you.

Within minutes, I was struggling. I initially thought it was just a touch of lethargy brought about by the cold night. The climbs were intensifying, and I was starting to dehydrate. I didn't want to hold Sam up, so I told him to go on. He'd been very kind—stopping to let me catch up—but I was now trying to walk too fast for my skills. I eventually told him to go ahead and that I'd see him later. A couple of other hikers had scheduled a shuttle for Dick's Creek Gap at 3 o'clock, and I didn't want to miss it. Consequently, I allowed my poor decisions to pile up by not stopping for either food or water in my desperation to get there. By the time I arrived at the pick-up point, with about ten minutes to spare, I was absolutely spent. I had hardly enough energy to drag my pack off my back and heave it up onto the back of the truck. I cursed my own stupidity and I rarely, if ever, missed breakfast again.

We had been greeted at the pick-up point by a quiet guy driving the shuttle. He worked for the hostel that the other hikers were staying in, so he charged me $5 for my lift. I gratefully handed over the cash. The way I felt, I would have gladly parted with my firstborn to get to the Holiday Inn, so five bucks was eminently reasonable to me. Mind you, he was clearly a man of unimpeachable integrity, as he regarded his duties fully discharged at the hostel, and unloaded me and my companions. I was still three quarters of mile from my lodgings, a distance I couldn't even contemplate at that moment. After a bit of man-to-man negotiation, he agreed to take me on for another $5. However, as he was now freelancing, he felt obliged to use his own vehicle. At least this was my interpretation of our negotiations. He actually only grunted most of the time, but I'm fairly quick on the uptake, and moved my gear into his truck.

It was an interesting vehicle that looked as if its interior had been hand-painted orange, though I believe it had originally been a garish red. The truck wasn't in the best condition, boasting a winning combination of sweat, cigarette smoke, and extreme flatulence. Additionally, it contained an assortment of unfinished fast-food meals that looked to be several weeks past their best. There was literally not one inch of carpet or floor mat to be seen, so completely was the junk distributed. My new friend spoke not a word and, when I looked at him, he seemed to be a touch deficient in the neck department. His beard appeared to start at his ears and ended around his chest. It was as if his head was attached directly to his shoulders by this matted growth. I could hear distant banjos in my mind, and decided that he wasn't up for conversation. Anyway, I reasoned, there are only so many ways in which you can interpret a grunt.

Ten minutes later, I was happily, exhaustedly, and finally in my room. I have been lucky enough to have stayed in many fine hotels in my life, though few have been as welcome to my soul as this one. The carpet retained the vast majority of its original color, and the bathroom fixtures, towels, and sheets were all an unrelenting white. There was the added bonus of a high-definition TV, operated by a remote control that didn't fall apart immediately in my hands. The Wi-Fi worked flawlessly, and there was a coin laundry just down the corridor. Oh yes, and I could also see through the window. Bloody heaven.

I was slumped, motionless, and thinking how dumb I had been. This was an impression that Diane liberally endorsed a few minutes later in a phone call. I confess that a conversation confirming my utter stupidity wasn't precisely what I was after, yet I knew she always only ever said things out of love and concern. I let it go without too much comment.

Having regained some equilibrium, I called reception to find out if there was decent restaurant nearby. I was directed to Daniel's Steakhouse, literally just around the corner. I dressed as smartly as a hobo can, then hobbled the short distance. The bad news was that it wasn't a steakhouse, though the very good news was that it was an A.Y.C.E. buffet. The acronym—meaning All You Can Eat—was probably the finest combination of four letters on the trail. These places attracted hikers like ticks to a deer and were highly desirable. Exactly what the proprietors of these places thought when a bunch of shabbily dressed eating machines showed up and shoveled down pounds of food, I can hardly imagine. The two New Hampshire girls who had spent the night at Woody Gap on the floor of the bathroom were there, so I joined them as they finished their meal. While it was always fun to compare notes with fellow hikers at the end of the day, serious eating needed concentration, dedication and, frankly, hoggishness, so I only got stuck into the buffet after they left. I returned to the trough several times, and the hunger pangs of the day were banished.

The day had made me think seriously about my actions. I realized, while walking back to my hotel, that I had been lucky to have gotten this far without being all that smart with my choices. With only 70 miles under my belt and another 2,100 to travel, I knew that this charmed life wasn't likely to continue unimpeded. At this stage of the hike, I was expressing the mileage as a percentage of the overall total, so just over three percent hardly registered. There were going to be far worse days, and I would face more extreme challenges. It was my responsibility to take control of my decisions, and to weigh them against my ability to achieve the goal of the day. Until this point, I had been going with the flow, spending far more time in towns and not enough in the forest. I was going to stop next in Franklin, North Carolina, and, quite apart from my delight at crossing the border, I was looking forward to reconnecting with the forest for the next four days. I resolved to take my day as another teachable moment in a sea of teachable moments and try to retain the lessons. I eventually drifted off to sleep in those unquestionable sheets. Marvelous!

The Holiday Inn provided its inmates with what it referred to as a continental breakfast. For me, this entailed two massive scoops of scrambled egg, a biscuit, and at least 15 rashers of bacon. I quickly demolished this, and followed up with a couple of slices of toast, plenty of butter, and two hefty dollops of strawberry jam. Despite the prospect of an easy day, I knew that hunger was not going to be a factor. Conversations with my fellow hikers, both the night before and at breakfast, confirmed that all had experienced a tough day after Tray Mountain. Most of us seemed to be taking it easy and were heading for Plumorchard Gap Shelter, a mere five miles ahead. There were some steady ups and downs, but these weren't too taxing. I was pleased that it wasn't just me who was feeling it, and I set out with a full stomach, happy to be on the road again.

I was by myself and stopped for a leisurely lunch, sitting on a tree trunk while I prepared and ate my mayo-and-salami wrap. I shot a video to reassure my wife that I wasn't in immediate danger of fading away. Quite how a 245-lb man was going to achieve that magic feat was beyond me. Several youngsters passed by and, waving them on, I was content that the hike was largely going to be this way. I'd come across people *en route*, but would rarely hike with them. I was okay with this, because I'd meet some of them later in the day at camp. I also recognized that I would be meeting a changing cast of characters. Early friends would become fading memories, as I introduced myself to their replacements. It turned out that I'd meet several of these youngsters at various times later in the trip. So much did they vary their pace, and rest stops, that even I was able to catch up with them.

In my guidebook, Plumorchard Gap Shelter was noted for having a stump in front of the shelter that had been a home for copperhead snakes. While I was becoming slowly accustomed to seeing snakes, I was happy that I hadn't encountered any copperheads so far. Snakes always made me jump, whether a harmless black one or a rattler, and I was never thoroughly comfortable around them. As you'd imagine, when I arrived at the shelter I immediately checked out the stump to see if any of the little devils were present. Concluding that this was a copperhead-free zone, I nevertheless set up my tent behind the shelter to get as far away as possible from the stump. The shelter was one of the nicer ones that I saw. I even considered staying in it for a short while, but the stump was unavoidably close, so back to the tent I went.

Such a short hike had allowed me to get there in the early afternoon, so I pulled out my "chair." It was a neat contraption that allowed me to convert my sleeping pad into a very comfortable lounger. I took the opportunity to read for the remainder of the day while the sun slipped slowly in the west. The chair was actually one of the items that I had been advised to leave behind when I attended a meeting of the Florida Appalachian Trail Club just before starting out. Wiser heads than mine had cautioned against taking it. However, I'd stuck with it and, with this first use, I felt that I'd been justified in keeping it. I was reminded once more of "Hike Your Own Hike" and laughingly gave the proverbial bird to my friends at the Florida A.T.C.

Chapter 11: On the way to Franklin

It felt like a rare luxury to be able to sit and read in the sun; a special treat to be savored with pleasure. Eventually, however, the needs of the hiker took over and I had to replenish my water supply and cook my evening meal. Plumorchard's water source was on the trail into the campsite. I was able to meander slowly to it in the dwindling sunlight.

At the source I found the delightful Simba, one of the fearless young girls on the trail, happily washing her feet in what was becoming a growing bubble bath. I mentioned that this wasn't supposed to be a public bath house—more in jest than anything else—and she blushed mightily. I think she had genuinely not considered she was doing something wrong, so we spent about ten minutes clearing the bubbles away. I very quickly got to love the taste of mountain stream water and found that, with this one exception, everybody took care not to pollute water sources. We all washed in streams, but made sure we were downstream before doing so. I'm fairly certain that Simba didn't make the same mistake again.

I used the word fearless to describe Simba. She was one of a number of similarly strong women who saw the trail as a place to be celebrated, where they were treated, even judged, on the same basis as men. Interestingly, as the number of hikers thinned out over the course of the next six months, it was my experience that it was the women who tended to stick at it more than the men. At Springer there appeared to be about four or five times as many men as women. Such a disparity was reduced throughout the following six months, with men dropping out in greater numbers. It was thrilling—awe-inspiring even—to see these terrific young girls kick ass as powerfully as men. Not only was there Simba at this stage but also Stylze, Twist, Tigger, Bluebird, and, later, Voodoo and Popeye. Each could more than hold her own in this tough environment. One of the western world's strengths is the way in which women are empowered. The emerging countries will never be able to compete until they unleash the talent of their women.

When I started my hike, about 70 or 80 miles back at Springer Mountain, I knew that hiking through, then out of, Georgia was going to be a challenge. I also felt that when I left

Georgia, I would have stepped up to the next rung of this long, arduous ladder. This wasn't just because Georgia was regarded as one of the tougher southern states. It was more because I would have proved to my doubters that I was capable of living in the wild and that I was serious about doing this. To be frank, I was one of the doubters.

All my life, I have started projects that flared for a short while before fizzling out in a blaze of indifference. I refer to these projects as enthusiasms. One of my earliest enthusiasms was golf. I have always been sporty and took up caddying at a local course in the U.K. at the age of ten or 11 to earn extra pocket money. The job was effectively child slave labor, requiring me to haul a heavy golf bag around a course, then paying me a paltry sum of cash at the end. I remember that the fee for a caddy was seven shillings and sixpence—about 60 cents—for a four- or five- hour round. I would often carry for two rounds in a day.

Despite this inauspicious start, I had been given an introduction to a game that has lived within me for years. I was also lucky enough to try my hand at it at that early age. Usually, kids who start a sport at a young age tend to become proficient if they stick at it. Not only did I stick at golf but I integrated it into my business life, playing all over the world. I played some of the world's great courses in England, Scotland, Ireland, Spain, Japan, and America, though rarely progressed beyond, at best, a 15 handicap. While I can still thump the ball huge distances, my skills are best described as adequate, all of 50 years after I started. Even though I have played for the majority of my life, I have never put in the work to get much better.

Playing the piano and writing are other enthusiasms that haven't produced the results I was hoping for. I decided, as I entered the '90s, that I would take up the piano as one of two resolutions for that year. The second was that I would publish a book before the turn of the millennium. To be fair, I didn't specify which millennium. I was newly married—for the second time—and looking for some life changes. I bought an old piano and set up a bunch of lessons with a local teacher. For a couple of years, I made some progress. Then, when it got too difficult and required a bit more dedication, I stopped. I didn't play much for the rest of the '90s but, divorced once more, I took it up again and treated myself to a gorgeous new piano for my apartment in London. I made some progress and when I moved to New York City, my piano came with me. I am now retired and, with so much time on my hands, I should try to step it up a gear. But 25 years after I played my first tentative notes, I am no better than an intermediate pianist, at best.

As for the writing, I've at least started with this book, though many years after my initial target. Whether or not I'm any good, I suppose time will tell.

I also took, and dropped, Japanese lessons for my frequent business trips to Tokyo. Some people even used to refer to my penchant for collecting wives, and girlfriends, as something of an enthusiasm on my part.

My point is that crossing the border from Georgia to North Carolina was a critical step for me, allowing me to prove to myself that this wasn't an enthusiasm. I worried that my friends and family were expecting me to fail. More importantly, I worried that I was expecting to fail. Simply putting one foot into North Carolina out of Georgia changed all that. While I still had a huge distance to cover, I was no longer afraid that I wasn't going to do this.

The border sign itself was something of a disappointment. The spot was marked by a piece of wood nailed to a tree on a long, arcing escarpment. The letters *GA/NC* were carved neatly into the wood. I would have breezed right past it if there hadn't been a couple of people standing there taking pictures. I stopped and took a couple of my own, with a selfie in Georgia, then one in North Carolina.

Georgia had been fairly severe, especially for me, a newbie. North Carolina and Tennessee boded well as less intense hikes. That was the theory, at least, but the first major climb turned out to be a hideous, almost vertical climb up Sharp Top. This had looked like an innocuous hill in my guide, yet my pumping heart told me otherwise, working ferociously to take me over this peak. I was reminded once more that the guide couldn't be relied upon to reflect upcoming horrors, and I decided that this was probably a good thing. It was only when I was really into Sharp Top that I became aware of its intensity; knowing that in advance wouldn't have made it go away.

Looking at the topography depicted in the guide as straight up and down was also misleading. All that I saw was a two-dimensional representation of the hills and valleys that showed at, say, mile 79.1, that I was at 4,300 feet. Each tenth of a mile would thus have a higher or a lower elevation, showing ascents and descents as smooth. The reality was far different. There was a richness in the variety of the climbs and dips that couldn't be replicated on the guide. To continue the example above, mile 79.2, just a tenth of a mile farther on, may have shown 4,350 feet. That would suggest a 50-foot climb in that tenth of a mile. However, I could have easily dropped 250 feet, then risen 300 feet to achieve that. While the guide pointed to interesting variations on the trail, it didn't prepare me for the constant change in elevation and the attendant assault on my muscles and breathing.

As with virtually everything else in life, it is only by experiencing something that you get a true idea of what it is like. I had expected the two-dimensional version of the trail. What I experienced was a far more nuanced and layered version that never bored me. On the other hand, it taxed me far more than I had ever imagined.

Sharp Top was soon a distant memory as I crossed the rather inelegantly named Chunky Gal Trail, finishing the 12-mile day at Standing Indian Shelter. The gorgeous, though still cold, weather continued. As soon as the sun dropped behind the mountain, everybody retired to their tents or settled down in the shelter.

Mice were always an issue at the shelters, and I'd become used to them while eating there, or simply hanging out. Most hikers would hang their food every night on bear cables. These could have just as easily been renamed mice cables, for they helped protect our supplies from the ever-present nuisances. There were necessary accommodations that came from living in a wilderness where we shared space with the natural inhabitants. We adopted an almost feral way of life without consciously doing so, acclimatizing to our surroundings as a natural response. I was surprised by the ease with which this happened, though a little concerned as to how far the trend might continue.

Of immediate concern in this regard was my stop the following day. The plan was to get into Franklin in two days from Standing Indian Shelter. Stopping at the first shelter would have meant a short day and too long a journey the following day. However, pushing on to the second shelter would have been a 20-mile day and very few of us were ready for that at this stage. We needed to find a campsite somewhere between the two shelters, and Betty Creek Gap was the obvious choice.

My worry was that there was no privy and I would be forced to face that worst of all fears, for me, of crapping in the woods. My wife had bought me an orange trowel for this very purpose at Christmas. The trowel hung proudly, and currently unused, from my pack. Being a creature of regular habits, I knew that I was going to be putting it to use the following morning, almost certainly before sunrise. I dreaded it. That night, with premium space somewhat limited, a group of about a dozen of us set up among the thick foliage, encroaching into the woods. It really felt like a camp and everybody gathered around a fire to warm themselves and discuss the day. I pulled out my chair once more to a bit of playful ribbing, though I'm sure I noticed one or two envious glances.

Naturally, given my worry about the absence of a privy, my system decided on a wake-up call when the sun was still tucked up in bed, and the night air was cold and dark. I tried to delay the inevitable, but by 6 o'clock there was no alternative course of action. I grabbed my orange trowel, plus other necessary items, donned my headlamp, and left my tent. The night was searingly dark as I headed away from the campsite. I chose to wander back up the trail to find my own little patch of forest beyond any potential spectators. This was as much for their benefit as mine. I moved off the path and headed about 30 yards into the woods, finding my spot. I must say that, had I not wanted to go prior to this nighttime walk, I would definitely have wanted to go now. I should also mention that digging a hole to bury your waste is probably the antidote for any guy who likes to take his leisurely time at his business.

While it wasn't precisely the way I'd like to spend the rest of my life disposing of my bodily waste, it wasn't as bad as I had feared. Another barrier—however minor—had come down. Returning to camp, my friends even gave me a small round of applause, as I proudly shared with them this unqualified success.

Betty Creek Gap had been something of a revelation for me. I had not only overcome another of my silly fears, but I also felt part of this young, open group that had built up. Acceptance as a peer was important to me, and this was given willingly. I recognized that we all met in camp, or at shelters, with the same level of achievement under our belt. We all knew how tough it had been to get there and we wanted others to succeed, just as we wanted ourselves to succeed. None of the lessons I was learning were anything other than positive.

I was carrying this positivity as I left camp, which was just as well, because I was soon to come up against Albert Mountain, another seemingly innocuous climb, yet by far the steepest terrain we had seen to this point. It was at the 100-mile mark and, despite the toughness of the incline, I loved it. There was plenty of hand-over-hand stuff that made me reminisce about my childhood in Wales. I used to scramble over rocks with my brothers, while my mother shouted at us from below to come down. At the top of the mountain, there was a fire lookout tower that provided me with my most spectacular views so far. As always, I tried to record this stunning scene with my iPhone. Yet it was the image burned on my retina, then stored in my brain, that far exceeded anything that Apple could provide me with.

I needed to move on, for I still had another ten-mile trek to get to Winding Stair Gap. From there, I was going to get a shuttle into Franklin. The path was relatively easy after the initial descent from Albert Mountain and I enjoyed the rest of this warmer day. My enjoyment leapt up several notches when I came upon my speedier friends relaxing at Rock Gap, and tucking into a Trail Magic feast. This was an earlier gap than the one I had intended to finish the day at, and I feared that the day was pretty much over for me.

An ex-marine had set up at the gap, with the plan of heading north at Easter and completing his own thru-hike, which he had started the previous year. Every hiker was getting two hot dogs, with the works, along with unlimited cans of Coke. After four straight days on the trail it was a heightened treat, ultimately proving, as I had suspected, to be the end of my hike for the day. I took the opportunity to enjoy the moment, then got a lift into Franklin from the marine.

The day had been terrific, with a mix of both easy and tough hiking. The icing on the cake was meeting this selfless man, who simply wanted to help his fellow hikers. Moments like that just amplified the feelings of friendship, kindness, and unity that were constantly apparent on the trail.

Chapter 12: Thoughts on my kids

It had taken me nearly two weeks to hike just over 100 miles to Franklin. I knew that I would need to up the pace substantially to finish somewhere near my hoped-for end-date of September 25 or 26. While I was happy with the progress I was making physically, I was still troubled by some of my thoughts. Most of the tougher ones centered around my two sons, Rob and Pete.

I had left their mother and, by extension, the two of them, in 1986. We had not had a happy parting, and the fact that I was leaving for another woman was a hurdle too difficult to cross. I'm sure that both my sons and I have differing memories from that period. Both sides are valid, as I've always been aware that somebody's perception is his or her reality. As a consequence, whatever I thought was happening at that time, and whatever they thought was happening, truly was taking place in our own minds. I respect their truths too much to try to change them, yet the scars remain, for all of us, from this divorce.

I remained in close contact with them, regularly taking them for a Saturday or an entire weekend. I remember those painful Saturday mornings. I would collect them for the day from their mother's house, and our first stop would be McDonald's. If you're divorced, you'll recognize this scene. Looking around me in those early days, I was astonished how many single dads, plus two kids, were occupying the place. I used to say that McDonald's could easily reconfigure their restaurants by installing tables that had one seat on one side, and a double-seater on the other. All the dads looked miserable, while the kids were eating unhealthily and often unhappily. If we were honest, we were looking forward to 5 o'clock, when we could return our sad charges to their mothers. The children just couldn't understand why their parents weren't together, and wanted everything in their world restored.

The relationship between my kids and my second wife—the first Diane—was always problematic. There was huge resentment, many times fueled by their mother, though also exacerbated by Diane's attitude towards them. She had two children of her own and flagrantly favored her kids over mine. As her husband, I was caught in the middle of this tension—

rightly so, because I caused it—but I always tried to maintain some balance. I'm sad to say that I would fail more often than not. The boys grew harboring this resentment, both to Diane and to me. The three of us managed to maintain our precarious relationship through those early years, and even through the tricky teenage years.

Rob, my elder son, was a very articulate, very confrontational young man. He would often want to argue on a variety of issues, knowing just how to tweak me and choosing to do so regularly. When he was about nine or ten years old, we had to call a halt to our rough-and-tumble "fake" fighting in the hallway of my home. Diane had noticed that he was lashing out at me and that it was starting to get out of hand. She was right, and I put it down to a simmering resentment, so that had to stop.

Pete was almost the polar opposite to Rob. He was far quieter, gentler, and appeared to be happier in his own skin. He maintained an equanimity that I was grateful for, given Rob's more combative nature. Underneath this was a steely stubbornness that he controlled well in those earlier years.

Because Rob was constantly challenging me, he commanded a lot of my attention. That seemed to infer to family and friends that Rob was my favorite, even though that was never the case. I loved, and still love, my sons equally.

Given the difficult relationship that my boys had with my second wife, I tried something on their eighteenth birthdays that looked like a good idea at the time. When Rob turned 18, there were regularly seven young adults in our home. Diane's daughter, Jenny, usually had her boyfriend staying with us, while her son, Dan, had his girlfriend sleeping over. Rob and his girlfriend were often there, plus Pete. While this could be fun, flash points regularly occurred. I suggested a way out to my wife.

I would buy Rob an apartment, putting 40 percent down as a deposit. I would also arrange and guarantee a mortgage. Once Pete was 18, I would—and later did—do the same for him. My motives were various. I was hoping to get the boys on the property ladder and felt this would be a responsible way to start. I was also effectively removing some of the tensions in my home. Third, quietly, I was trying to redress the balance of favoritism that my wife's children had enjoyed.

It was not an unqualified success.

I often had to make the mortgage payments, and both apartments quickly deteriorated. Neither son paid much attention to protecting this investment. Rob once jokingly told me that this was how an 18-year-old was supposed to live. Eventually, and almost inevitably, the apartments were sold, my sons were off the property ladder, and the substantial profits went who knows where.

Growing up as my sons may have been tricky for my boys. It wasn't that I was so wonderful; indeed, far from it. However, with both boys leaving school at the age of 16, they needed to find work. With an increasingly competitive environment, the only realistic way they could find a decent career, absent appropriate qualifications, was in my industry. In those days, my ego, drinking, and relentless womanizing made me a less-than-perfect parent and role model, but my sons saw a lifestyle that had certain attractions.

From the outside, I had plenty of money, a great apartment overlooking the River Thames, and a successful career. The problem was that the three character defects noted in the previous paragraph eventually conspired to bring about my downfall.

When Rob and Pete were looking for employment, I was able to smooth the way to get them into junior, but promising, positions. Neither was especially suited to the insurance industry, and both were unwilling to put in the hard work to develop themselves. I recall once that Rob, in an outburst of anger, told me that he didn't just want to be *like* me, he wanted to *be* me. That was a terribly hard thing to hear from my son.

None of this was healthy, but I tried my hardest to give my boys a head start. Looking back, my drinking was the thing that skewed my version of reality. What I hoped was helping was only fueling additional resentment. We would meet up for lunch in the city, share a drink and a meal, yet I should have known something had to give.

Eventually, it did.

On March 9, 2004, when I least expected it, my life suddenly hit a brick wall. I had been working for a Bermudan company since 1994. I had been employed as the Principal U.K. Executive—or P.U.K.E., as my colleagues would occasionally refer to me. My role was to develop a new account, and build a permanent London presence for the company. I achieved this after a period of commuting between London and Bermuda for about a year. The business grew and, by 2003, it was a large reinsurance operation in the London market. A senior manager had been sent over to run the whole enterprise in the late '90s, though he eventually planned to return to Bermuda.

At that stage—and I may be flattering myself here—I was one of only two people in the London office likely to be considered for the senior position. The role didn't go to me and, given my earlier confessions, it isn't difficult to see why. As a consequence, with seniority settled, I had to marginally moderate my lifestyle. However, the decision only exacerbated tensions between me and this new manager.

Then, the axe fell.

I had a meeting scheduled early that morning in March 2004. My secretary told me that the boss wanted to join the meeting. He came in our office and walked straight into the meeting room, with a thunderous face. I ambled in, ahead of the appointed time for the meeting, and said "Are you okay? You look really pissed off." He replied, "We need to have a serious discussion." It may give you some idea of how unsuspecting I was when I thought to myself "Oh my God, they're getting rid of Bren." Brendan was my deputy, and I knew that this manager was looking to cut costs across the board. Behind me, I heard the door close. I turned slowly to see the Human Resources manager joining the meeting. It was *me*. They were getting rid of me. In an instant, it all made sense. Frankly, I would have fired me too.

They handled the whole process extremely professionally, but it was all I could do to concentrate while my future was shattered in front of me. They were paying me an excellent severance, as well as vesting some shares that netted me a fair sum of cash, yet it was over. That life was gone, seemingly for good.

This isn't supposed to be a memoir, though I wanted to give some context to what happened next with my kids. Left comfortably off—at least for a couple of years—I started a consultancy business, involving myself in the lucrative world of reinsurance arbitrations and expert witness work. I took a month out to tour Italy with my then-girlfriend, Jo. I even bought an old farmhouse in Umbria along the way, so erratic was my lifestyle.

The drinking didn't stop; in fact, it increased. I became a kind of human relay baton, getting to the city at 1 o'clock for a two-hour lunch. Seeing pals on the way, I would arrange to meet them after their lunch, or after work. In this way, I'd be passed on at 3 p.m., then at 5 p.m., before stumbling home, as drunk as a skunk, at virtually any time of night. I was a mess.

The tension with my sons also increased and, just before Pete's twenty-first birthday, in September 2004, it snapped. I had arranged to drive the 40 miles down to their home town, Southend, for dinner with the two of them. I told them to order drinks and snacks because I wasn't sure what time I'd get there. By the time I arrived, they had taken the opportunity to get a few beers inside them. Rob became very aggressive, and we allowed ourselves to get dragged into a daft conversation about a 9/11 conspiracy. Pete just sat back, tuning out, as we went at it. Suddenly, Rob leaped up, pushed a few drinks off the table, and headed for the door. Passing behind me, he allowed those years of frustration to surface. He started punching me on the back and side of my head. After six or seven blows, he stormed out. I was more stunned than anything else and just sat there as Pete stood up, announced that he was "fed up with this fucking family," and walked out. Rob soon apologized, but Pete's stubbornness was unrelenting. Pete and I haven't spoken a single word to each other since that moment.

A lot more happened over the years to bring about this simmering resentment, some real and some imagined. Whatever the truth, I knew that apologizing to my sons was more important, and lengthy, than my previous apologies to my wives. One of the qualities I've admired so much in a number of my friends—and you know who you are—has been their complete commitment to their children. Many have drunk as much as I have, several have taken drugs, and some have behaved badly towards their wives. Despite these shortcomings, their children have remained at the center of their world. I wanted to make that commitment—I really did—but I'm afraid that I lost that battle early on in my first marriage. On the trail, I wanted my boys to forgive me for the harm that I had wrought upon them. I had carelessly sacrificed their happiness for my own baser instincts.

Since I have been able to control my excesses, I have reestablished what I believe to be a strong relationship with Rob, my son. He knows that I love him unconditionally. Even better, he has found some happiness in his own life I thought he would never get. Nonetheless, Rob deserved an apology and got a very fulsome one on the trail.

Pete doesn't know I've apologized, and he may very well never know, or even care. What I hope he discovers one day is that he was, and is, loved and valued. I have tried over the years to reach out to him on many occasions but with no success. If he ever reads this, I can assure him that I will always welcome him back in my life. Strangely, the son of a friend of mine ran into Pete in a bar in Thailand a couple of years ago. He took some photographs and emailed them to me. Pete refused to smile, instead adopting a deliberate scowl. I stared at those pictures for hours, trying to make out what was going through his head. I realized that—ten years on—Pete was a man I didn't know. I desperately wanted that to change.

Chapter 13: Franklin to Nantahala Outdoor Center

Another uninspiring motel in Franklin was my home for the night. I shared a very funny evening with Sam—recently named Muffin Man—Simba, Jay, and another young guy, Boss Man. Simba was only 19 and unable to drink alcohol, though she managed to sneak a few slurps from my beer when the inattentive waitress wasn't watching. Despite the Trail Magic session earlier, at which we had all overindulged hugely, we were ready for chicken wings and burgers.

The youngsters, untroubled by my need to record mileage on as many days as possible, had decided that the following day was going to be a "nero" day. A "nero" was defined as a not-quite-zero day, meaning just a few miles hiked. They were going to watch a movie in the afternoon, then head out just before dark. After the Trail Magic earlier, they had gone beyond my stopping point, so they only needed to cover just over 4 miles to get to Siler Bald Shelter.

Listening to them discussing the choice of movie over their wings and burgers was hilarious. They were debating whether to see *Noah* or *The Muppets*, hardly contiguous along the spectrum of movies to watch. Both films were discussed with an appropriate solemnity that reflected their desire to find the one that best fitted their mood. I'm not terribly sure what their eventual choice of *Noah* said about their mood, though the choice was unanimous.

When we returned to our motel, with many hikers in attendance, word got around that the First Baptist Church in Franklin was offering a free breakfast in its church hall the next day. The church was sending a coach at 7:15 in the morning and all hikers were invited to attend. Now, I'm aware that America, despite claims of a separation between church and state, is considerably more religious than my more secular home country. That said, I suspect that the need for a second coach the following morning had more to do with the prospect of copious amounts of pancakes and bacon, than a desire to listen to God's word.

The place was packed out. In a trip that had already been overwhelming due to the kindness of strangers, this was another heartwarming—and belly-filling—moment. Volunteers herded us towards the food and coffee, encouraging us to come up for seconds. We were also asked to add our trail names to a space on the wall to become part of that ministry's history of helping hikers.

But the biggest, and to my mind the most Christian act, was the distribution of writing paper, with the promise to mail our letters home, wherever "home" might be. Such a warm gesture immediately had the effect of reminding us all of home. We were given the space to re-connect for a short time, as we sent our love to our families. Each hiker had been photographed when we arrived, and the photo was returned, to be added to the envelopes with our letters. It is hard to describe how important this was to me. I also know that my wife treasured both the note and the photograph. Both remain affixed to the fridge in our kitchen. Apparently insignificant actions sometimes have an exponentially larger impact than even the perpetrator is aware of. I just know that this was an early highlight for me that resonated for weeks.

Once breakfast was over, we were bussed back to the motel and shuttles were arranged. I was now a bit grumpy, knowing that the others were heading back to where they had left off the previous evening, while I was the only one who had bailed out at Rock Gap. As always in life, and especially on the trail, it had been my choice, so I was responsible. I was mainly ticked off because bad weather was forecast. Consequently, I set off with a heavy heart and an expectation of rain in the very near future. The sky was doing nothing to disabuse me of this notion, nor was the radar on my phone. Yet, despite these ominous threats, the day remained mainly dry, with just a few drops of rain from time to time.

From Rock Gap, the trail went up and over an unnamed hill, giving me a climb and descent of about 700 feet to Winding Stair Gap—the traditional stopping point for Franklin. The gap was also the place where most of my friends had started, or would start, after their movie. I felt that I was beginning my day at this point, and steadily climbed the four miles to the turning for Siler Bald Shelter, set at 5,000 feet. I wouldn't normally take a half-mile side trail to a shelter, but this was the place to stop. There was a moderately gentle blue-blazed trail down to a drab shelter that redeemed itself by having a covered porch. This welcome addition allowed us to eat and hang out in the dry, watching the weather deteriorate outside.

Another barrier was removed at Siler Bald, for I slept in a shelter for the first time. The wind was starting to whip up and, with the threatened rain seemingly imminent, I took the plunge. I had imagined before the A.T. that everybody would have similarly bad habits as me, yet, in general, I found this not to be the case. However, in this shelter—chosen as my first— everybody snored beyond belief. They also punctuated the snoring with regular bouts of extreme flatulence. It was as if we'd all agreed to an unspoken competition that rewarded the person who could reach a new level of noise and anti-social behavior.

Two of my roommates in this shelter were a married couple, though they were both wed to somebody else. They had teamed up early in the hike and appeared to be as compatible, possibly more so, than most married couples I know. I found this arrangement odd, though it certainly looked like it was working well for them. I was still at a relatively early stage of my hike, and would see similar, entirely asexual couplings later in the hike. The couple complemented one another, and their goal was to take their partnership to Katahdin. I often wonder how that worked out.

Of the two other occupants in the shelter, one said virtually nothing all evening. What he lacked in vocabulary he more than made up for in his snoring prowess later. The other guy was a very funny and somewhat ethereal man in his early 30s, named Hemingway. This was the first time I had met him, but he turned up at various times later in my hike. He seemed to transport himself from place to place, rather mysteriously, because I hardly ever saw him actually hiking. Hemingway had his very own style, quite unlike most hikers on the trail. He sported a magnificent cap that wouldn't have looked out of place at a smart shooting party in Scotland. Also, he always wore a tie. Indeed, he had three ties with him, one for every occasion. He was a keen exponent of the fragrant cigarette, with one constantly hanging loosely from his lips. On this evening, he told us that he had taken an accidental detour into camp, and, instead of a half-mile walk, he had taken a nine-mile odyssey of his own. How he managed to rack up an extra nine miles I couldn't totally understand. I think the cigarettes may have added a touch to his confusion, yet his demeanor suggested that he was perfectly at ease with this additional, unnecessary effort.

Eventually, despite my concerns about sleeping in the shelter, I settled down. Naturally enough, I was immediately serenaded by the cacophony I had expected. My wife tells me that I snore—and I certainly don't doubt her—though I find it hard to believe that I could have competed with this group. It was awful. I didn't sleep a great deal, though clearly more than I thought, for there was an extra body in the shelter when I woke the following morning. Apparently, the youngsters, having watched *Noah*, extended their dinner, then purchased flaming torches from Walmart, hitting the trail in the dark like Indiana Jones wannabees.

I loved this sort of derring-do and, even though I wasn't the type to try it, my admiration for these fearless hikers went up another notch. They were grabbing the chance to make this the adventure they wanted, and I loved to see it.

I planned to get to Nantahala Outdoor Center in two days. Cold Spring Shelter was pretty much the halfway point and my target for day one. However, with nobody in any hurry to move the following morning, I lingered over breakfast, setting out far later than I had intended.

I think that if there had been one lesson I could have learned prior to this trip, it would have been that starting early on the trail had benefits far beyond expectations. Somebody later referred to "ten by twelve," meaning that he wanted to get about ten miles hiked by noon. The afternoon was then far more relaxed with those early miles under his belt. I was terribly slow to pack up, have breakfast, and get going for the first two or three months. Had I simply followed the "ten by twelve" rule, I think I'd have finished a month earlier.

It was a morning of uninspired hiking, with much huffing and puffing, though minimal progress. Sometimes I simply couldn't kick myself into gear, and this was one of those times. When these negative days happened, I would often look for a way out. Even though I had been hoping to get to Cold Spring Shelter, the guide showed me an alternative. If I stopped at the shelter before, Wayah Bald, I'd have to put in my longest stretch—16 miles—to get to Nantahala the following day. So I cut my losses early, paid attention to my screaming and creaking body, and took the short path to the shelter. As I had expected, there were no other hikers, so I at least had the opportunity to grab a nice flat spot and set up my tent before settling down to read in my chair.

I spent two hours in perfect silence, with the watery sun keeping the chills away. I was just considering the nervous possibility that I would be by myself for the coming night— another first that I was eager to avoid for the time being—when a couple of hikers turned up. They were joined later by several others, all of whom were new to me. Having enjoyed the solitude, I was grateful for their company at dinner that evening. Camping alone was a joy that I was able to delay for a while.

At this point I'd like to mention something about hiking itself. With no previous experience, I had rapidly learned lessons on the fly. The main lesson at this stage was just how glad I was that I had brought trekking poles with me. Astonishingly, at least to me, some people made do with no poles at all. Such a decision suggested to me that they either had the balance, or the brains, of a mountain goat. Given my painful early experiences, I tended towards the latter. Every step that I took threatened potential calamity, with the careful placement of both poles and feet critical to success. Even with this additional support, I continued to fall on the trail with alarming regularity. Terrain varied dramatically from state to state, with rocks and roots providing hikers with the sternest of tests. Rain added to the mix made both lethal. How I would have negotiated these without poles I couldn't imagine.

Another early lesson was that, despite the beauty all around, watching my feet for most of the time became central to the health of my toes. When I started, I had stubbed them on rocks at least 20 times a day. This was evidenced by the fact that the majority of my toenails had turned black and would later fall off. In planning my hike, looking at my feet for over 2,000 miles hadn't been one of the things I had considered.

With a 16-mile day ahead me, the following morning I experimented with my calorific intake to try and give myself a boost to reach my goal. I'm not sure if it was the difficulties I'd had the day before, but for the first time I entertained doubts that I had what it took to complete this journey. I was disappointed in myself that I'd shortened the hike, as I had been left with a long trek into Nantahala. Unfortunately, I think I'm fairly lazy by nature, so I knew I needed to watch out for this if the whole enterprise was going to stay on track. My real fear was whether or not I'd be able to put in the big days necessary in Virginia. I had been stuck around the eight- to ten-mile mark for most of the hike so far, while people were speaking about 20- and even, God forbid, 30-mile days. I simply didn't think the 30-milers were within me, while the 20-milers seemed something of a stretch as well.

Oatmeal is the ubiquitous breakfast on the trail, though it can become a little tedious. I felt it needed something of a makeover to balance taste with calories. There was due to be a supply of food from Diane at Nantahala, so my flavoring supplies were limited. Choosing a couple of peanut butter pots, I mixed them in with my oatmeal. You might think that this would be revolting, and probably won't be surprised that you'd be correct—it was awful. However, it gave me the boost I wanted. I covered four miles in the first hour and a half, really getting into my stride. Then, a long uphill stretch hit me hard, and I staggered up Wesser Bald to find a spectacular observation tower at the top. It looked like a great spot for lunch and a breather, so I took the opportunity to rest, eat, and regroup. Peanut butter on a wrap was the only option in my depleted pack, so I gratefully wolfed that down. The dazzling view from the top of the observation tower, followed by this burst of calories, re-energized me. The last six and a half miles were a downhill stretch into Nantahala. Though my knees took something of a battering from this extended, unrelenting, downhill stretch, I reached my goal after my longest hike. I should have been elated by this achievement, but the doubts still nagged at me.

A shower, followed by beer and a burger, among a large bunch of hungry, chatty hikers boosted my confidence once more. Several of my fellow travelers had also questioned themselves, so I just pulled myself together and regrouped. We were down at just over 1,700 feet and due to climb up over 5,000 feet the following day. I was actually looking forward to it.

Chapter 14: On my way to the Smokies

I woke the following morning in my bunk room, discovering that I was sharing with somebody who had obviously arrived later than me the previous evening. I hadn't heard him come in and had slept like the dead. When I noticed that he was stirring, I ventured a neighborly, and jolly, "Morning" to introduce myself. He grunted "Morning" straight back at me, so we chatted a touch before he turned round. I'd just asked his name and, as he moved around in the bunk, he muttered "Blackbeard." Never has a trail name been more appropriate, or more obvious. What greeted me was a perfectly black, bushy beard that made the wearer look as if he'd eaten a black bear, and was just stuffing the rear end into his face. I must have looked startled, but he just smiled when I said, "Suits you."

Given that people were constantly meeting strangers, a trail name was an important part of a hiker's persona. These names usually served as the first point of contact, and were often thoughtful if chosen by the hiker, though rarely complimentary if chosen by others. I was always struck by how different Mighty Blue was to Steve, and I embraced this change. It wasn't that I had anything against who I was back in real life, I just enjoyed presenting a new version of myself.

Even though I was glad that I hadn't left my naming to the wit of others, I managed to "christen" a couple of people myself. Greg was one of the group of younger men and women—Muffin Man, Simba, Wing it, Tigger, etc.—with whom I had traveled from time to time. He was a fairly serious young guy in his mid-20s, and was referred to by his given name for the first 100 or so miles. One day, while hiking alone, a trail name came to me.

Greg was an undeniably well-informed guy on pretty much every topic that came up. He would spout facts that nobody could possibly refute, given the detailed nature of much of the information. He could opine on the relative virtues of single malt whiskeys and crafted beers, then would instantly pivot to the best available tents and backpacks for hikers. He seemed to have an encyclopedic knowledge of, well, virtually everything. I found this to be especially strange in somebody so young. I was musing on this and suddenly came up with a trail name that fit the bill. The name was marginally, though playfully, chiding, though also appropriate. If adopted by Greg it could be seen as self-deprecating. The trick was not only to suggest it to Greg in a non-insulting way but also to have his buy-in to adopt it. It certainly wasn't my intention to upset him, though I was aware he could be offended.

That night, it had been at Betty Creek Gap, I was sitting around with friends and told Greg that I thought I'd come up with a good name for him. Gamely bracing himself for an insult, he smiled and waited. "I think you know so much about pretty much everything that your name should reflect this encyclopedic knowledge." He looked unsure as to where I was heading, so simply smiled again while I continued. "Given that, and given the modernity of the younger generation, I thought 'Wiki' might be a good name." Everybody thought it was hilarious while Greg, in his serious way, considered it. He said, "Yes, I suppose I do know quite a bit." So Wiki was born, without feeling insulted. After that, I always felt a little proprietorial about Wiki's progress.

It would be about another 1,200–1,300 miles before I was able to contribute to another hiker's trail name.

A name which mystified me until it was explained, was for a lovely young Texan—another of the fearless young women—named Stacey. She was referred to as "Stylez." I assumed that the name had something to do with fashion, for she walked rather elegantly. I later learned that she had been a ballerina when younger. One night, she cleared up the origin of the name by explaining that the pStyle is a device for women to pee standing up. My innate British conservatism was slightly shocked by this revelation, so she demonstrated the use in a sort of dry run, so to speak. Who knew? I'd got to the age of 60 without knowing women could do this. Frankly, I didn't feel much better for knowing that they could.

A couple of others in this early group were Twist and True Story.

Twist was accompanied by her scrappy dog, Oliver, on the trail. She was a very private woman, named Kim, and went by her own name for the longest time. Oliver turned out to be such a star, while she was more laid back. She became more associated with him than he was with her. Eventually, somebody tied the two together and they became Oliver and Twist.

True Story must have set himself up early as such, for everything he said was prefaced by "True story" as he launched into a tale. When I got to meet him, he had moderated this personal tic, but not before the name had irredeemably stuck.

The morning at Nantahala Outdoor Center presented the slower hikers, like me, with something of a conundrum. The weather looked lousy, the forecast was for worse to come, and there was unlimited food and beer to be had by staying exactly where we were. Such a winning combination was, for the youngsters, precisely what they were looking for to see out this grim day. A zero day was nothing for most of them. For several, it seemed to be better than hiking, and most were intent on taking advantage of the goodies on offer.

While I didn't fancy the thought of slogging uphill for the first six miles from 1,750 feet to over 4,200 feet, I couldn't bring myself to abandon the day so airily. So, with my British attitude towards the weather very much to the fore, I perceived a small break in the clouds and took my chance. Inevitably, within 15 minutes and several hundred feet up the mountain, I was proved to be woefully over-optimistic as the heavens opened once more.

When the rain subsided, I experienced something I'd never even imagined before, let alone seen. The day was still cold and, with the wind whipping around the tall, swaying trees, small ice flakes were dislodged and fell to the ground. These created a brilliant ice storm that tinkled out of the startlingly blue sky. At first, I confused it with snow. However, the clear sky above told me that it couldn't be so. Peering above me, I could see that it emanated from the tops of the trees. At times it was comparatively powerful, almost emulating a mild hail storm. I had another new experience under my belt.

The rain and ice required me to change in and out of my wet-weather gear several times. This was always an exhausting and sweaty process that was exacerbated by extensive climbing. Temperature regulation, both hot and cold, was such a tiresome issue on the trail and I never worked out the optimum use of rain gear. I suppose my only satisfaction was that other hikers appeared to be similarly conflicted.

That night, after an exhausting hike, I descended gingerly down to Sassafras Gap Shelter, constantly aware of the wet, mucky path. Despite this attention, I must have relaxed only steps from the shelter, falling heavily, and very muddily, to end my uncomfortable day. I had been just cold and wet prior to the fall. I was now cold, wet, and covered in mud, which put a weary punctuation mark on the day. I stripped off my foul clothes in the shelter, and gratefully pulled on warmer clothing. That at least allowed me the luxury of setting up my tent in relative comfort. Believe me, in this context, at this stage, relative comfort was a wonderful thing.

I was now so ready for bed that, after a brief dinner, I said my goodnights and headed for my tent. It was still early but I was done. I'd fallen, I'd been soaked, both from sweat and from rain, and I'd climbed endlessly. I also hadn't done any laundry in about five days, so warm certainly didn't mean clean.

Settled, exhausted, and snug in my sleeping quilt, though smelly, I suddenly recalled that my food bag was in my tent. Normally, I'd have rectified this basic error by jumping up and hanging it on the bear cables, but today my heart just wasn't in it. *Sod it*, I thought, *I'll chance it. I've been soaking bloody wet all day long, walked uphill for most of the day, and I'm not getting out of this bloody bed just in case a flipping bear comes by and smells something in my pack that he fancies.* I improvised, wrapping my foul-smelling socks around my food bag, then settled back down. If a bear could detect something edible over that stink then I felt he was probably welcome to it.

My smelly socks must have worked, for I woke up the following morning utterly uneaten by bears. I even felt a bit smug, as if I had cheated death. It's funny how small victories can take on an elevated status in these circumstances, when, in reality, I'd been lazy and foolish. There is a reason that bear cables are provided at shelters. Those who ignore them do so at both their peril and the peril of those around them.

I was trying to get to Fontana Dam in a couple of days. On my guide, this looked to be trending downhill for the first day, though my first steps would lead me over 5,000 feet as I crossed Cheoah Bald. From there, despite a few ups and downs, I would finish at Cable Gap Shelter, at less than 3,000 feet. All this seemed eminently doable, even though it amounted to a 16-mile hike, equaling my longest day so far. What the elevation guide hadn't shown me—though it had been mentioned at the shelter the previous night—was that we would be going up and over the infamous Jacob's Ladder. This was a climb of 700 feet that had to be negotiated in about a third of a mile.

It was truly horrendous, with the path rising steeply at every stage with no switchbacks to ease the pain. I was stopping every 20 yards or so to breathe deeply, though I managed a quiet smile to myself as I passed a young guy on the path. I rarely passed a soul, so overtaking any human was an achievement for me. My smugness was punctured a little as he then sped past me and mentioned that the Yankees had won the previous evening; he had been checking sports scores on his phone as I had passed him. "Go Yankees," I said, ruefully.

With every climb you eventually get to the top. When you do, it is a transitional moment, with those burning muscles released to sulk by themselves. The summit of Jacob's Ladder was wonderful to reach and I sat to reconsider the guide. What looked like a tiny blip in the topography had turned out to be a heart-pounding, leg-screaming, endurance test that wasn't even mentioned in the guide. I wondered what other surprises I had in store over the next 2,000 miles, but concluded that not knowing was actually to my benefit. As if proof were ever needed, I reverted to my normal approach to life. Basically, this entails only worrying about something once I have to face it head on. Until an issue confronts me, I try not to preempt it.

My rest at the top of Jacob's Ladder revitalized me and, even though I looked longingly at the next shelter as I passed it, I finished the final six miles at a good pace. I fell asleep that night with my confidence and strength enhanced by the day. With only a relatively short hop to get into Franklin, I felt very much at home in the woods.

My short hop turned out to be a tough early climb, followed by a knee-jarring descent that plagued me over a prolonged period. The first flowers of spring were emerging, but I found it hard to concentrate on anything other than placing my feet and mitigating the painful effects of such a sharp descent. I could see Fontana Dam for several hours before I finally staggered on to flat ground. There was an information office at the bottom to greet hikers with some unwelcome news: I had hoped that the shelter was nearby, but learned of another mile-and-a-half climb that didn't ease my pain. Having watched the target for such a long time, this bonus climb didn't improve my mood.

Desperate to get the day over with, I set out immediately. A man of similar vintage to me, Sherpa, was just ahead. We chatted for a few minutes, and would see one another several times over the next couple of hundred miles. However, there would then be a gap of about 1,500 miles before we would meet again. By that time—in Maine—he had grown a beard so luxuriant that I didn't immediately recognize him, so drastically had he changed. I was always delighted to run into old friends whenever, and wherever, they showed up.

The Fontana Dam Hilton was supposed to be the smartest shelter on the trail. To be fair, that was a low bar to breach. Most shelters were simply three wooden walls, open to the elements at the front. Sometimes there was a tarpaulin to pull across the front to dent the impact of high winds, though most were open to the elements and provided scant protection on the harshest nights. The "Hilton" was different, in that it boasted a fourth wall, though there was still an opening for the wind to rush through. The shelter wasn't set deep in the woods, and it even had an approach road that accommodated cars. With a memorable view of the dammed lake, it was certainly the prettiest shelter I'd seen to date. However, I had a strong urge to shower and freshen up my clothes, so I decided to ditch the "Hilton" for the Fontana Lodge, located nearby, in Fontana Village Resort.

I shared a cab to the lodge with a couple of fellow hikers, though they were more interested in the lunch that had received such a good write-up in the guide. Booking a room at the very reasonable price of $60 for hikers, I was reminded that those of us who were able to afford to stay in town more regularly were probably having an easier time of it on the trail. I eased my conscience by pointing out to myself that I was over 60. Playing the old-git card, even to oneself, normally covered most bouts of conscience.

My room was warm, clean, and private, with working Wi-Fi and HD TV. Happy days! I felt very relaxed to be settled in by the early afternoon, and ambled down to the restaurant. A gaggle of hikers had gathered, in search of yet another burger-fest and a couple of beers. With the Smoky Mountains lurking just across the dam, we all enjoyed the break before our next adventure.

The inevitable result of beers and a burger was a quick nap back in my room. My thoughts then turned to laundry. Almost inexplicably, this facility wasn't provided by the Lodge, and the nearest spot was a trudge of about a mile downhill. With no available cab, I set out and got to the town center, comprising a laundry and the Fontana General Store. Both buildings were doing brisk business and I had to wait to get my laundry started. Several friends were there and, with nothing else to do and nowhere to go, we hung out in front of the store, chewing jerky and chewing the fat.

Most of the youngsters were staying at the shelter so, once my laundry had dried, I said goodbye and backtracked to the motel. I changed into my least-foul clothes and hit the restaurant once more. I had a leisurely, quiet dinner, with wine and relatively fine dining. I felt refreshed and ready to start my adventures in the Smokies.

Chapter 15: The Great Smoky Mountains 1

Rested and fed, but slightly thrown by the strangely deserted Fontana Village, I faced the Smokies with growing anticipation that I would soon see a bear.

Thus far, my animal count had been extraordinarily underwhelming, with a noticeable absence of anything terrifying. There was even a dearth of non-threatening animals that I would have expected to see in the woods. By my calculations, I was about 160 miles into the hike, and had thus far encountered four squirrels and a deer, along with several mice in the shelters. I think that if you'd asked me before the hike what I thought I would have seen by now, that haul would not have been my pick. 40 miles per squirrel was a tad disappointing; I could have seen more of them by simply walking around my gated community in Florida for about 30 minutes.

Bears and snakes were, of course, a step up in wildlife from mice, deer, and squirrels, so I was disappointed not to have seen too many of these. I had seen a couple of harmless black snakes—which always made me jump—with their slithering resolve to get away from humans as soon as possible. I never felt threatened by a snake on the trail, although I treated them warily when I did see them. I also don't care how tough you think you are—a snake is going to give you a frisson whenever you see one.

The Smokies' reputation promised a whole new level of wildlife, so I was really pumped to make the climb, literally, to new heights. I was going to be moving up from the dam at 1,700 feet to over 4,500 feet and Mollie's Ridge Shelter on that first day. After that, I'd continue upwards to Clingmans Dome, the highest point on the trail, two days later.

I was entering the Smokies on a Thursday morning. My plan was to cover about 40 miles to Newfound Gap by the Sunday morning, cadge a lift into Gatlinburg, check into a motel, and wallow in the final round of the Masters, my favorite golf tournament. To get there on time, I would need to achieve my goals. The first one—that climb of nearly 3,000 feet on the first day—was critical to making it on time. I'd learned that plans can quickly fall over if you miss your goals, so I was determined not to allow this to happen.

Luckily, the weather was co-operating beautifully on that Thursday morning, and I set out from the "Hilton" under a warming sun. The dam is an inspiring sight as you cross it. At 480 feet, it is the highest dam east of the Rocky Mountains, serving hikers as a curving and inviting introduction to the Great Smoky Mountains National Park, that looms ever closer as you approach it. Walking along a concrete road was also something of a novelty, and, while I appreciated the flatness, I missed the unevenness and give of the trail.

Like many previous mornings I was alone, though I could see a young guy, Stealth, about 800 yards ahead of me. He was named Stealth because he was extremely quiet, unassuming, and pretty much kept himself to himself. He would seem to materialize in a crowd, apparently from nowhere. He was also reputed to be quite the guitarist.

As I left the dam at the north end, the road started to rise slowly, and I was soon looking for white blazes once more. At the appropriate point, the trail took a left turn, off the approach road, then headed into the forest. There was a $20 fee to hike in the Smokies, and my wife had paid this online for me, mailing me the required paperwork to deposit in an honesty box on the trail.

The trail at this point widened a bit, and I had a wonderful, tiring trek to Mollie's Ridge Shelter. I hadn't seen any bears, but I was in the Smokies. That, as I reflected, dozing off that night, was very special indeed. The next day also had a singular significance to me, and I looked forward to making a video to record it, somewhere around Mineral Gap.

While this hike was my own journey, I had always had a kind of sub-plot that I wanted to explore. My problem was sharing this sub-plot with others, because the chances of me completing this hike were, at best, 50-50 and at worst, long odds against. My inexperience had no real context into which I could compute my chances, so I just assumed that improbable would be a fair bet.

That is not to say that I couldn't do it; I was trying to be realistic when taking everything into consideration. The fact that there had been fewer than 500 successful thru-hikers over the age of 60 was a touch daunting. This was especially so since most of those must have had at least some prior hiking experience. Let's face it, what sort of idiot takes up hiking for the first time over the age of 60? Even more barmy was the notion of a first-time hiker tackling the entire Appalachian Trail in one go. However, I felt that I had a bloody-minded determination that would carry me quite far, and, in my quiet moments, I thought that I could do it. Indeed, that elite group of 500 people was one that I dearly wanted to join.

I have been on the board of a local child abuse prevention agency, the Family Partnership Center, for a couple of years. I had discovered a charity that touched me sufficiently to get heavily involved. I wanted to conflate my hike into something of a fundraiser for the center, but I was wary as to when I should announce this. It would have been mortifying to have amassed several thousand bucks of sponsorship, only to quit on the approach trail because I simply couldn't do it, or, worse, if I couldn't stand it. Carrying the expectations of others is a heavy burden, never more than when you're carrying that burden into totally unknown territory.

Consequently, I came up with the idea of the *Last 2,000 Mile Challenge*. The idea behind this was that, at mile 185.3, I would have exactly 2,000 miles to go. I was hoping that people would sponsor me for a penny, a nickel, or a dime, per mile, so the calculation would be simple. I'd also have had the advantage of seeing if hiking suited me. I figured that with nearly 200 miles under my belt, I would have proved to myself that I could not only do it, but I would have resolved whether or not I was enjoying it.

I had suggested the idea of doing the hike about two or three years before with my friend Dave Potter, a slightly abrasive, though kind-hearted, Bostonian. At that time, he was the executive director of F.P.C. I tried to frame it that the hike was still unlikely at that stage, but that I wanted to make the attempt. By the time everything came together, and I was in the process of selling my business, Dave had retired. I was happy to let the new executive director of the agency, Katrina Bellemare, into my plans. Katrina is an extraordinarily empathetic woman, whose heart is totally invested in the charity's mission. The fact that she is also an outstanding executive director is a blessing to both local families and those of us on the board.

I was, consequently, somewhat committed. However, I still wanted to avoid making the effort public until there were only 2,000 miles to go. In much the same way that my plans on the trail would change at a moment's notice, this plan hit something of a wrinkle prior to my departure, though it was certainly a welcome wrinkle to have.

I had been speaking with one of my old mates, Chris Clark, from the U.K. Chris was a business contemporary who grew up with me in the insurance business. We have shared a solid friendship for over 30 years. Friendship has its privileges, one of which is to abuse, or tease, each other mercilessly. To say that Chris had doubts about my ability to hike the trail was something of an understatement. He had seen me in my 270-lb days and certainly didn't imagine me as a likely candidate for such an exhausting trip. Chris owned a holiday home in a golfing community nearby, and we were chatting in his home—it must have been six weeks before I left—when I told him about my plans. He was well aware of my F.P.C. involvement, having generously sponsored me previously in a golf tournament. Once he had stopped laughing at my ridiculous plans, he said that, in the unlikely event that I completed the trail, he would give $1,000 to the charity. This was a payment, as he told me, that he never expected to have to make. With such a wonderful start I began to feel that burden of expectation gnawing at me.

To compound matters, Chris was also at a dinner held at another friend's home in the same community a few weeks later, at which there were several other relatively wealthy guys in attendance, along with their wives. Discussion turned to my upcoming trip and the wives became engaged in not only the mission of F.P.C. but also the romance of the hike. So, I had the empathy of the wives and the cynicism of the guys. That mixed a heady brew, and elicited a total of $4,000 pledged, up from

Chris's original $1,000. I suspect that the renowned British capacity for alcohol may also have helped boost the total.

I wanted the video about the challenge to appear in my blog from the exact point at which I had 2,000 miles to go. A couple of miles short of Mineral Gap, I had passed over the spectacularly gorgeous Rocky Top, and wished that this had been the place to make the announcement. The sun was beating down, the wind had subsided, and the whole world was at peace with itself.

Unfortunately, the world rarely cooperates as we would like, so there I was, at an unprepossessing spot that my GPS divined as mile 185.3. I opened the *Last 2000 Mile Challenge* to my blog followers, taking the opportunity to pitch it to others in the hope that it would elicit a response. The results were gratifying. With that terrific start augmented by those pennies, nickels, and dimes, along with a presentation on my return, we raised just under $10,000 for the Family Partnership Center. While the hike was mainly my adventure, I couldn't help thinking that if I'd had more confidence before the hike, I'd have raised a whole lot more cash for a great organization. Nonetheless, that aspect of the hike gave me so much delight that I couldn't berate myself for this lack of confidence. I was grateful for those who bought into my enthusiasm.

Having made my begging video, I continued from Mineral Gap to Derrick Knob Shelter, only three or four miles ahead.

The shelters in the Smokies were a significant step up from those in other areas along the trail. Most had a covered eating area and many had a fireplace. They were generally larger than other shelters and had a ridge runner keeping an eye on them at regular intervals. There was a ridge runner on this night. He would stalk up and down his section to make sure that a certain amount of order was maintained and trash was kept to a minimum.

There was a strict rule in the Smokies that no tenting was allowed if there was room in a shelter. To complicate this further, reservations could be made in the Smokies, so a hiker could be asleep at, say 11 o'clock, and another hiker could appear and claim his spot in the shelter. I didn't see that happen, and we were all highly amused when told this by the ranger. The thought of a hiker voluntarily relocating at 11 o'clock simply because a day hiker had turned up was hard to imagine. Precisely how this rule would be enforced I never had the chance to find out.

I was still on target to watch the Masters when I left the shelter on the Saturday morning. The previous day had been a 12-miler, while this day would take me up Clingmans Dome. At over 6,600 feet, it was the highest point on the entire Appalachian Trail. I would then hike to Mount Collins Shelter that evening, leaving me less than five miles the following morning to Newfound Gap and the road into Gatlinburg. It was going to be a 13-and-a-half mile day. I was now getting comfortable in tackling these longer distances, having been stuck at around ten miles a day, or even less, for about three weeks.

Another gorgeous day gave us some stupendous views along the way, with much of the hike along undulating ridges. At one of these open, rocky tops, I ran into four day hikers enjoying a break. For no apparent reason, one of the men in the group gave me a couple of sweet candies and, not wanting them at that moment, I stuffed them into an accessible pocket in my backpack. None of this group were sucking candies, and I was a bit nonplussed by this random generosity, though the gesture came back to save me later in the day.

Leaving the group after a rest and a chat, we started to go down for several hundred feet before a long, curving climb up towards Clingmans Dome. I was hiking with a young man named Boss Man, who was excellent company, and we chatted amiably through the day. As the approach to Clingmans Dome became steeper, the forest grew increasingly thick, to a degree I hadn't experienced before. The whole space seemed almost primeval. If ever I expected to be mugged by a bear, this was the spot. There were all sorts of noises and apparent movement in the undergrowth, but nothing appeared.

We passed a huge tree that had been blown down, and its base, with the exposed roots, was now perpendicular to the ground and about 15 feet in the air. Once again, we were in awe of how spectacularly violent and majestic nature can be. It was tough to comprehend the force needed to uproot this magnificent tree, which lay there, its roots defiantly reaching back into the ground for sustenance.

Continuing the climb, we could hear voices near the top. Feeling sure that such a tourist attraction would have access to water, I gulped down the rest of my second liter and emerged onto the asphalt path circling upwards to the observation tower on Clingmans Dome. The tower was built in 1959 and, while it rises only 45 feet above the mountaintop, the circular observation platform is accessed via a spiral ramp that is 375 feet in length, and rises at a twelve percent grade, syncing with the Clingmans Dome Trail leading up from the car park below.

Suddenly, we were amongst people, and I felt unnerved by this unwanted exposure to the world outside. The day was sunny and clear, promising extended views all round, so the observation platform was attracting a large number of visitors. Many of these visitors looked as if this approach trail was as much exercise as they would get all year, so heavily were some of them puffing while they heaved their 350-lb frames up the path. A few looked as if they had recently consumed their own personal banquet.

While I couldn't help but feel smug about my presence, I'm sure many of these visitors looked at us and simply rearranged the letters of the word smug to express their own opinion. That said, once we had made it to the top and taken the obligatory pictures, several of these visitors engaged us in conversation. They were fascinated by our adventure, and I admonished myself for being so judgmental.

To my dismay, I could see no access to water and I realized that I would have to hike the remaining four and a half miles to the Mount Collins Shelter without any, for there appeared to be no streams on the way. Knowing this made me panic a little, though there was simply nothing to do other than get on with it, so I set off. Several hundred yards into the climb down from the top, with my mouth getting more parched every step, I recalled the candies in my backpack, so I hastily retrieved them. They were fruit sweets and luxuriously juicy, so much so that the saliva was soon flowing freely once more as I relished every suck.

I had often heard the expression "the trail provides," and so it proved on this day. My more religious friends would see this as evidence of divine intervention, and I certainly saw it as strange when I was handed those candies earlier in the day.

However, the idea that a God could foresee me running out of water later in the day and provide me with sweets to slake my thirst, struck me as being beyond ludicrous. I'd have thought that somebody who pays such attention to detail might consider something a touch more beneficial to mankind, such as eradicating leukemia in children, for starters.

The last of my candies dissolved in my mouth as I took the short side trail to camp. I asked for the water source and was directed to a stream 200 yards down a steep path. Rushing to it, I filled my water bottles, pausing to drink a liter before refilling once more. A stream never tasted so good.

I'll always remember Mount Collins Shelter as the place where I saw my first wheelchair-accessible privy. While discussions regarding privies are hardly riveting, it is worth noting that all new such buildings in state-sponsored national parks were required to be wheelchair accessible. What some of these people in Washington are smoking when they come up with these rules, I just can't imagine. While I'd encourage everybody to get out in the open air, there is absolutely no way that a wheelchair user could use the Appalachian Trail and, by extension, the privies thereon. Sometimes you wish that a modicum of common sense would prevail.

Chapter 16: Gatlinburg

An easy five-miler the following morning to Newfound Gap on US 441 left me still above 5,000 feet with the weather rapidly deteriorating. A few hikers had gathered to try and hitch lifts, and a very amenable mother and daughter scooped a bunch of us up. They bundled four of us, with our backpacks, into their car.

I found on the trail that so called "trail towns" were populated by the kindest people. They would go out of their way to leave a good impression with hikers, extending a helping hand when requested. None of us knew the addresses of where we were all individually staying, so our angel simply drove up and down streets in Gatlinburg to find everybody's motel or hostel.

I ended up at the Microtel Inn and Suites. By 1 o'clock, I was happily lying on my bed, remote control in hand, and gearing up for the Masters. That is what I call hiking.

With Bubba winning his second green jacket, I felt that it was time to celebrate with—what else—a burger and a few beers.

I don't know if it was just that I was getting attuned to being in the woods and away from civilization, but I can't imagine that, at any point of my life, I would have liked Gatlinburg. It was probably great if you wanted to get a tattoo, terrific if you were up for a day in Dollywood, and awesome if you wanted to visit Ripley's Believe It Or Not. As I would rather have poked myself in the eye with a sharp stick in preference to these activities, Gatlinburg wasn't really working for me. One thing that Gatlinburg offered in abundance, however, was the opportunity to people-watch, on both a large and terrifying scale.

My conversations with the receptionist at the Microtel suggested that she knew her way around, so I asked her for the town's best burger. She unhesitatingly directed me a few blocks away to Shamrock, an Irish pub that, happily for me, chose Sunday evening as its karaoke night. I set myself up comfortably in a corner, chomping on my burger and glugging a couple of beers while the place started to fill up with Gatlinburg's finest.

There appeared to be a glut of 50-year-old women, most of whom were noticeably absent a ring on the third finger of their left hand, though several had one through their nose. There was also a bunch of men in their 40s who conspicuously wore wedding bands. You'd have thought that Brad Pitt was in attendance. The women flirted, pirouetted, and generally fawned over these men as if the Last Days were around the corner and they needed to settle the deal immediately.

A few of the guys took the stage in an effort to impress and, screeching and lousy pitch notwithstanding, they seemed to enhance their stature with their acolytes. Through all of this, there was no trouble, no nastiness, and a tremendous amount of goodwill in the bar. I soon reined in my cynicism at these people simply having a great Sunday night out. Having come from an urban upbringing, it was always a revelation to me to see rural existence, even though Gatlinburg qualified as a town. What were the locals to do? Visit Dollywood again? Be amazed at the wonders of Ripley? They already had more than their fair share of tattoos, so karaoke on a Sunday night was right in the ballpark.

Yes, when I'd entered the bar I'd been laughing at them. By the time I left I was laughing with them. There is a big difference, and it was another part of my education on the trail.

Having surrendered most of the previous day to Bubba, I still needed to run a few errands. I was hoping to get these done before lunch, but, by starting late, I ended up having my first zero day. Diane had sent me a package that needed to be retrieved from the post office and I was in urgent need of clean clothes, so I decided to check both those boxes and added a haircut to the list.

Having to do the laundry meant heading out in a pair of swimming shorts, and my waterproof jacket. I figured that these were the only things that could prolong the wait for a wash. Completing the look were a pair of wet shoes that cost $9 in Walmart. When I tell you that I didn't look at all out of place in this ensemble, you'll understand something about Gatlinburg.

My new friend at reception helpfully mapped out a route, introducing me to the local transportation system of trolleys that moved people around. I'm not desperately good at following instructions, but everything worked like a dream. The first stop was to a barber shop in a strip mall heading out of town.

The barber couldn't have been more than 25, looked like a thug, and was covered in tattoos; he was clearly into Gatlinburg. As soon as I sat in his chair, he turned out to be witty, intelligent, and caring, talking lovingly of his girlfriend and his son. I'd imagine that several minutes hovering over me with his clippers made him understand that the laundry was sorely needed and shouldn't be delayed a moment longer than necessary. As he re-established my Yul Brynner look, he said he'd be happy to run me to my next two stops. Closing his shop, he drove me first to the post office, waited as I picked up my box from Diane, then dropped me at the laundry. He even offered me his phone number in case I'd like a lift back later. I refused it, while thanking him gratefully for his generosity.

Never did I take such random gestures for granted, and never did I expect them. When they happened, they were delightful nuggets that enhanced my day. I hope that the many trail angels realized just how much we all, as a hiking community, appreciated them.

For some arcane reason, it took three trolleys to return to town, over the course of less than two miles. Nonetheless, when you have little to do, you needn't be in a hurry, so I just relaxed and slowly returned to my motel. My internal body clock enjoyed this slower pace, and I've noticed on my return that it hasn't returned to its former breakneck speed.

It was only about 1:30 when I got back, and that left me with the choice of simply lying on my bed for the rest of the day or looking for a local attraction that didn't involve needles, huge breasts, or the world's tallest man. I settled on going to the movies, checking for listings on my phone. *Noah* was playing in nearby Pigeon Forge and was due to start in about 30 minutes. Once more, my receptionist friend came to the rescue and ordered a cab. I was in my seat at the theater, with a Coke and a large popcorn, as the lights went down.

I've already referred to my lack of a religion, though I knew many of the nuances of Noah's story reasonably well. Consequently, it was somewhat jarring to see the inclusion of stone monsters into the mix, despite the fact that they were hugely entertaining. If they'd been part of the story when I was a kid at school, I think I'd have paid a bit more attention. Despite what I presume was a certain artistic license, I thoroughly enjoyed the movie. Afterwards, I headed next door to devour a huge rack of ribs before another trolley odyssey back to Gatlinburg.

The following morning the signs weren't good, with rain coming down in waves that promised snow at higher elevations. I met up with Sherpa once more, so we headed towards the Nantahala Outdoor Center, or N.O.C., nearby. There was a shuttle that would leave by 10 o'clock. I was eager to get on it, even though I had neglected to reserve a spot.

There were several no-shows, doubtless due to a combination of the wet weather in town and the possibility of snow in the Smokies. Sherpa sensibly decided to sit it out for a day, but I got on the ten-seater bus, sharing it with just the driver and two other hikers. The thought of another day in Gatlinburg was more than I could contemplate, even though the N.O.C. staff advised us only to hike if we were experienced. If you ever visit Gatlinburg, you'll understand why I took the risk.

As we climbed back towards Newfound Gap, the rain turned to light snow and I started to realize that I might have bitten off a little more than I could comfortably chew. The three of us got out of the bus and looked around. The snow was now coming down heavily, with the visibility no more than about 50 feet. I immediately recalled the advice back at N.O.C. and understood their concern. The temperature was projected to fall overnight to the teens, or even lower, and I was carrying a 30-degree quilt. I hadn't experienced a really cold night inside my quilt, because the quilt itself, in conjunction with the warming properties of the pad and the liner, had kept me comfortable.

The night was still to come, although the thought of a cold one stayed with me throughout my ten-mile day.

It was about 11 o'clock when I got off the bus. I was going to climb back over 5,000 feet, so I knew that the snow was  only going to get worse throughout the day. The other two guys left me behind fairly quickly, while I resumed my slow trudge through a thin layer of accumulating snow. I found out later that shuttles had been suspended for the rest of the day. This meant that I was probably the last person to hit the mountain that day. It was a realization that, given my inexperience and try-it-and-see attitude, I was in more danger than I was prepared for.

One great thing about hiking, technicalities notwithstanding, is that it is a case of putting one foot in front of the other for an extended period of time, and getting to your destination unscathed. *I can bloody well do this*, I thought to myself, and so it proved. I expected to take five hours, and I hoped to hike ten miles. Both were achieved, and I reached Peck's Corner Shelter at almost exactly four o'clock. The day turned out to be one that battered me constantly with varying degrees of rain, sleet, and snow, but I turned up at the shelter with another test passed and a feeling of achievement.

I was unable to bask for too long in this small victory, because far worse was to come.

Chapter 17: Back in the Smokies

The shelter was the only place for me that night. However, with less than capacity and a ranger in attendance, I would not have been allowed to camp even if I had wanted to. The wind picked up considerably as night fell, and we were grateful for the ranger's presence when he produced a tarp to fit tolerably well across the front of the shelter. The temperature began to plummet dramatically. Meals were taken in tense silence, with the storm whipping up around us. The ferocity of nature was evident from the horizontally swirling snow that we saw as we peered into the darkness. Everybody cleared up quickly and tried to settle down for the night.

It was, by some distance, the most frightening night of my life. I'm sure I've been in greater peril, and I've no doubt that I have been less aware of dangers around me. That said, this was an experience that hit me with a visceral reaction that stays with me today.

My quilt allowed me to cinch the top around my neck, effectively sealing me inside. For the most part, this would keep me warm. One night, a week or so before, I had cinched a bit too much, and almost garroted myself when I turned over in my sleep.

On this night, nothing would help. I was wearing my Mighty Blue woolen hat down over my ears and nose, trying, but failing, to keep them warm. I was cinched as far as I could go and was wearing almost all my clothes. In fact, the only clothing that remained in the bag were a pair of underpants. I had two pairs of socks, two T-shirts, my fleece, and another jacket, along with my waterproof jacket. My feet were like the proverbial blocks of ice. Nothing I could do would thaw them. The most worrying moment was when I felt that coldness creep higher up my legs. I felt like I was freezing from the feet up.

Strangely, getting up for a pee in the night turned out to be the best thing I could do. I was dreading it, but the inevitable happened at around 3 o'clock. I hadn't slept at all and simply had to go. Urgently dragging myself out of my quilt, I slipped into my camp shoes, and emerged into the night. It was horrendous, with the snow stinging my face like needles. Hikers were supposed to pee well away from the shelters, but I'm afraid I was going nowhere on this night. Indeed, I had to hang on to the wall of the shelter simply to stay on my feet while I urinated wildly in the air. Getting back into my quilt, something seemed to have relieved the tension, and I slipped off to sleep.

I woke about three hours later with my feet and legs nice and toasty. Looking around, somewhat chastened by the severity of the night, I could see the concern on other faces as we chatted about how cold it had been. One older guy, who told us he was 77, informed us all that he had been in the Arctic Circle a few weeks before to see the Northern Lights. He said that the temperature there had been as low as minus 20 degrees. He swore that the previous night had felt colder.

The ranger gave us a more realistic figure of mid- to high-single digits. I found out from hikers from Gatlinburg a few days later that the recorded temperature in our region, at that elevation, had been seven degrees. Whatever it was, I was grateful that the night was over.

The 77-year-old man was spending a few days hiking with his grandsons. They were 12 and 16 years old, and they did both their grandfather and their parents great credit. They were terrific kids, who worked as a team with their grandfather, and were willing to help in every way. I had been impressed how well young kids adapted to such harsh conditions, both in terms of hiking and weather. I had run into several Boy Scouts and others who had all been polite, hard-working, and respectful. If this is the next generation of leaders, then bring them on.

Unfortunately, the night had slightly ruined the Smokies for me. The first three days had been splendid, with each view topping the previous one, while the weather had cooperated perfectly. Gatlinburg had promised a deterioration and so it had proved. The views were now scarce, while the trail was frozen. Later, as the thaw set in, everything turned boggy. I found myself wanting to get out of the Smoky Mountains.

In the meantime, I had to cope with the newly frozen path and its inconsistent make up. I found it almost impossible to tell if the standing water was frozen until I'd committed to it. By then, it was often too late. I fell a couple of times, banging my knee so badly at one stage that I cried out like a baby. I was feeling a tad sorry for myself, and fast understanding my limitations for this hike. I soon came across my old friend of the previous evening, struggling manfully with his knees. As before, his grandsons were assisting him every step of the way. I'm sure that he fought on, happy just to be out with them.

The day had started with 23 miles of the Smokies to go. I had set my sights on Cosby Knob Shelter, which would leave me just over ten miles the following day to reach the legendary Standing Bear Farm. Despite the unpleasantness of the trail, this worked out well, although I found those two days to be a slog.

Eventually, the ice turned to slush, and then the slush turned everything to a muddy mess. I was grateful for my boots, keeping me warm and dry while sloshing through a trail that now required constant vigilance and attention to pole placement to avoid an undignified, mucky fall.

Starting out on the Tuesday had been an error. I had missed many gorgeous views, as everybody who started a day later took great pleasure in telling me. It goes to show that the views, when and where they are available, should be enjoyed for what they are, when they are. I was taught a further lesson about staying in the moment that I have tried to hold on to since my hike.

A last climb down and I was out of the Smokies. Even as a Brit, I'd heard of the Smoky Mountains. While researching my hike, I had thought they would likely be a highlight. That had certainly proved to be the case in the first half, with spectacular views, enjoyable trails, and even a better class of shelter. The second half simply reminded me of the capriciousness of the weather, and the impact that it can have on one's day.

Now that I've had some time to think more about the Smokies, I'd say that my feelings have softened. All in all, I had a wonderful experience hiking through this famous park. I still wonder how I managed to avoid virtually all of the wildlife while I was passing through, but that was only a minor irritation. On reflection, that may have had more to do with the fact that I was constantly looking at my feet in an attempt to avoid a catastrophic fall. Indeed, I may well have walked right past all sorts of animals that simply ignored me and went about their business. Several people suggested that these parks are so well-traveled that animals seem to know where the path is and tend to avoid it. Let's face it, the majority of us announced that we were in the vicinity by our food, our noise, and our own distinct smell. I would think that it would have been pretty tricky for wildlife not to know that a stinky hiker was around.

That last climb down, exiting the park, led me to a flat, smooth path that ran alongside a fast flowing river. This, in turn, emptied into Pigeon River, which I crossed via a road bridge. The drama of the Smokies was replaced by gentler hills, and a short uphill hike led me to signs for Standing Bear Farm.

This, according to both my guide and more experienced hikers, was apparently a "must go" hostel on the Appalachian Trail. For the life of me, I couldn't initially understand why. The hostel is located a mile or so from the end of the Smoky Mountains and I had heard it referred to as rustic. That could mean anything, particularly to a bunch of smelly hobos, one of which I had undeniably become.

My first sight of the place was less than reassuring, with a couple of extras from *Deliverance* sitting in rocking chairs, smiling at me as I entered the establishment. They couldn't have had more than half a set of teeth between them. The clearly senior guy, Rocket, introduced himself. I was struck by how he looked like a relic of the late '60s, early '70s, with his somewhat spaced-out look and laconic delivery. He had apparently been hiking through several years ago, landed at the farm, and never left; I could hear strains of "Hotel California" in my mind.

Later that afternoon, I asked Rocket how far away the nearest town was and the best he could do was, "We got a gas station 'bout seven mile thataway, an' I think anudder one 'bout 18 mile tha' way." "But where's the nearest town?" I insisted. After a pause, during which he thoughtfully stroked his chin, he conceded, "Don' rightly know," as if the thought had never occurred to him. Despite being geographically challenged,

Rocket knew everything about Standing Bear Farm, and he showed every visitor the various buildings that made up the facilities. The bunk room had about 20 beds, some of which were already occupied.

One guy, Cap'n Guts, came to the farm regularly for vacations, whiling away the time in this hippie paradise. He made us all laugh like drains later in the evening when he started to sound off about politics. That would normally be a subject to be avoided at all costs, yet there was no question that the majority of the hikers had a liberal bias, so comments abounded that tended to reinforce already entrenched ideas. Cap'n Guts, despite being an older, white guy, and bearing all the hallmarks of a Fox News aficionado, came up with a classic. "Now I'm not saying all Republicans are idiots—far from it," he started. "I know many very smart Republicans, so please don't think I'm calling them all idiots." He paused to take a swig of his beer. "It's just that I've never met an idiot who isn't a Republican." It hung in the air for a second, then the whole place erupted. His comment was so unexpected that I think that is what made it so funny to me. I laughed about it for weeks.

Connected to the bunk room was a communal area that had a few threadbare couches for residents to lounge on and generally chew the fat. There was no Wi-Fi because, as Rocket explained, he had converted the room that used to house the modem into a beer room. The room now contained a locked fridge, from which Rocket dispensed cans of beer at a very reasonable $2.50 a time. Precisely why a refrigerator would displace a modem was never actually explained, but I let it go.

There was a dining room that had a sink, a table, a stove, and a pizza oven. Attached at the back of this was the wash room, with a dryer, but no washer. There was a washboard in the sink, alongside a wringer—or mangle—but, since I had no idea how to use either, I had to forgo the pleasures of clean clothes for a few more days.

The last room was the store, or restock room. There was everything in here, from Snickers to pizza, both of which I bought among several other goodies. Unlike the locked fridge, this was offered on the honor system. We had to record what we took, then settle with Rocket in the morning.

None of the above should be seen as a complaint against Standing Bear Farm, as it all simply worked. I absolutely loved it there. The place was very companionable, and everybody had a very chilled time. At $15 for the night, plus purchases, it was a bargain. I'd been shown once more never to judge a book by its cover.

Chapter 18: On the way to Hot Springs

Having thoroughly enjoyed my evening at Standing Bear Farm, I slept well and left early the following morning. I was hoping to make Roaring Fork Shelter by nightfall, crossing Max Patch in the process. It was going to be a strenuous 15-mile day and I wanted to put my best foot forward.

Max Patch is a bald at over 4,600 feet. Balds are wild mountain summits, or crests, generally covered with native grasses or shrubs, in place of forestation. There are several theories as to why these places are devoid of trees, but no definitive answer. The romance and mystery immediately promoted balds as my favorite feature in the southern states.

Max Patch had once been cleared for pasture in the 1800s and appeared to be an anomaly, sitting high in the sky like a regular grazing meadow, instead of being the peak of a mountain. There were spectacular views all around, most significantly to the southwest, where we could look back on the Great Smoky Mountains and, turning to the east, the Black Mountains.

I had left that morning by myself, but quickly teamed up with a guy from Martha's Vineyard, named Digger. I was only with him for that day, but he gave me some of the most valuable advice I ever got on the trail. I had downloaded an app from Guthook Guides to my phone prior to leaving. The app used GPS to give me an accurate reading as to where I actually was on the trail, and how far I was from certain shelters or features, such as views and water sources. I had been stopping often and grabbing a breath, using my phone to check with the GPS to see where I was. Digger said to me, "Why do you keep doing that? The path is still going to be there, and the rhythm of your hike is interrupted, so why stop? When the path goes up, you climb, when it goes down, you descend—end of story."

He was absolutely correct. From that moment, I started to see my position on the trail as where I was at a particular point in time, instead of where I was going to be later. This prevented me from making these regular stops. My hiking speed became steadier, and, because I wasn't interrupting my rhythm, faster.

Digger also reminded me—though he was never aware of this—that the trail plays havoc with one's personal hygiene. We were chatting, walking close to one another, when I caught an incredibly strong smell that almost caused me to gag. *Oh my God, he stinks,* I thought. I slowly backed up until I was about 15 feet behind him. It was only then that I realized that the smell, still strong in my nose, was actually emanating from me. I chuckled quietly to myself and carried on, with a renewed respect for those who stopped and offered us lifts when we crossed roads. I also started to understand why drivers would always, surreptitiously, but definitely, wind down their windows when hikers were on board.

We made excellent early progress, even giving ourselves an extended stop for some spectacular Trail Magic. This was provided by Apple, who was apparently a regular on the trail. Donuts and Cokes gave us sugar and calories in abundance, so we pushed on, energized by these treats.

Digger was a faster hiker than me, but he moderated his pace to let me keep up. Approaching Max Patch, he started to pull ahead and got there about five minutes before me. It was gorgeous. As often happened on my hike, the weather was perfect when I crossed balds, and so it was on this day. I was able to let the 360-degree views sink in, my eye drawn constantly back to the magnificent Smokies in the distance.

I had been inundated with these new experiences over the first couple of hundred miles, and was desperately arranging them in my mind to make sure I could recall them. I failed on several, but Max Patch sticks with me as clearly today as it did at the time. The full magnificence of my surroundings was giving me a counterpoint to a lot of the ugliness of the world. I felt privileged to be able to see the undeniable evidence. Taking time to savor this beauty was very inspiring to me and, I'm sure, to those around me. Max Patch was also a spot that day hikers could reach, with a car park a couple of miles downhill. It is certainly a place I'd love to revisit someday, though probably from the comfort of the short walk up from the car park as opposed to the blood, sweat, and tears of the Appalachian Trail.

It had been a memorable day, albeit a long one. I reluctantly left Max Patch and headed down to Roaring Fork Shelter for the night. The shelter had apparently seen some lively bear activity, but nothing was going to disturb me that night. I set up my tent and slept for about ten hours. I felt like I had achieved something on this day, and that my hiking had stepped up a gear, thanks in large part to Digger. I still felt like a non-hiker, yet I was light years ahead of the know-nothing who had camped for the first time on Springer Mountain, only about a month before.

That night was the first time I'd slept in my tent for about five days and I embraced it. Strangely, I'd noticed that I was sleeping better there than in a motel bed and certainly better than in a shelter. My snoring remained an issue for me, even though, by definition, I'd never heard it. My wife's descriptions were sufficient for me to restrain myself from inflicting it upon others whenever possible. As a consequence, my tent was now my home, and would increasingly become my base in the months to come.

Unfortunately, with about 18 miles to go the next day to get to the quintessential trail town of Hot Springs, I got lost twice in the first couple of hours. This resulted in a frustrating hour or so correcting my errors. While I know that, in the general scheme of things, a couple of miles on top of my 2,200 miles should have been no big deal, it seemed disproportionately awful when looked at as part of an 18-mile day. It was also extremely disconcerting to hike for an extended period of time without seeing a white blaze to confirm that I was on the right path. When that did happen, suddenly seeing a blaze up ahead gave me extra energy and an almost irrational joy. By early afternoon, with the intermittent rain, accompanied by the constant getting in and out of clothing, I realized I wasn't going to make it to Hot Springs, so I moderated my ambition for the day.

I chose to stop short, at Deer Park Mountain Shelter, after a frustrating day of hiking. As I came to the shelter, I greeted the, as yet, unseen occupants with "I must have put on and taken off my clothes today more times than a bloody stripp..." when I saw a mother and three young children in the shelter. These were the delightful Foxworth family: father, Terry; mother, Nicole; Morgan, a deliciously innocent tomboy; the enchanting Signe, the fashion diva; and the rambunctious Rion, a very funny and sweet boy who engaged all in the shelter with his questions and general joy at his adventure in the woods.

A young guy, Cape, and I were sharing the shelter that evening, because the family had two tents between them. We were later joined by another, older guy whose name escapes me. We were royally entertained by the kids over dinner, and it was wonderful to be part of a family scene, albeit on the periphery. I was struck by the benefits of being out in the woods together as a family, if only on this four-day trip. It truly was a delight to meet them all, and I couldn't help but wish that I had had similarly adventurous parents when I was a child.

My childhood had been safe and happy. While these are certainly attributes you'd wish you could envelop your own children in, my folks never saw the need to expand their horizons. In fact, it wasn't until they were in their late 50s that they took the plunge and went to Italy on vacation.

I remember meeting them as they arrived back at the airport. My mother was glowing, gushing about Venice, and vowing to go abroad every year for the rest of their lives. "God knows what we were worried about; I wish we'd done that years ago," she said. Dad mentioned that mum had needed to rest some afternoons. They both put her tiredness down to the excitement of the trip and their crowded itinerary.

She was dead six months later.

She was diagnosed that November with a virulent cancer of her pancreas that decimated her body in a couple of months. The doctors had thought she had a gall bladder issue, so they opened her up with the intention of removing the offending organ on her fifty-ninth birthday. According to the doctor, they simply closed her straight back up, so complete was the grip of the cancer.

On the day of her death—expected, but still a dreadful shock—I recalled meeting them at the airport. I was grateful for the holiday they had shared, but I despaired at their truncated life together. My parents had always kept me and my brothers safe, and been cautious in their own lives. At that moment, this was both a blessing and a curse.

About ten years later, my father told me that he worried about me far more now that I was 40 than he had ever done when I was just four: "I knew you were always safe when you were younger; I just can't keep you safe now." I often wonder what dad would have said had he been alive to see me start this journey. I believe he would have recalled his holiday with mum, taken a deep breath, and wished me good luck.

The Foxworths had dragged these thoughts out of me. I dozed off to sleep that night, and my own rather checkered career as a family man came to fill my dreams with regret.

The sun rose the following morning in the perfect place to see the extraordinary things that sunlight can do to alter a forest. We were plunged in almost complete darkness when the first rays topped the mountains to the east. At first, it was only the tops of the trees that were painted in the golden light. Rapidly—like Tinkerbell—the rays darted in and out of sight, first lighting further down, then diffusing and illuminating different areas. Getting such a light show while I prepared my breakfast was a treat that never disappointed as I progressed up the trail.

Packed, entertained, and fed, I set off for the leisurely three miles into Hot Springs. I was fairly confident that another breakfast would follow the first in a couple of hours.

Nestled between two ridges in Western North Carolina, Hot Springs styles itself as the home of "Natural Hot Mineral Waters. Heated deep within the earth, these crystal clear carbonated waters are world famous for their mineral content and legendary healing powers." I'm sure all that is true but, for hikers, Hot Springs is the first real trail town that welcomes smelly hobos to eat and drink to excess. How the local tourist board balances these two dichotomies I couldn't begin to understand.

Entering the main drag through this small town of just over 500 people, my attention was drawn to the Smoky Mountain Diner on my left. According to my guide, this promised a spectacular skillet breakfast that I was looking forward to, having ingested little more than oatmeal for weeks. While oatmeal was certainly a decent way to shovel calories into my face at the start of the day, only eggs can make me feel as if I've actually had breakfast.

I was about to cross the road when I heard the shout "Mighty Blue" ring out from the porch in front of the diner. It was my young group of friends who I hadn't seen for about 100 miles. They all seemed pleased to see me. They had picked up a few stray hikers along the way, and were cozily grouped around one table putting a real hurtin' on plates of pancakes, eggs, and bacon. They all scooched up and found me space as I squeezed in.

Catching up with these youngsters, I noticed how much more mature they all appeared to be, having built their hiking minds, as well as their hiking legs. I also became aware that two of them had formed more than a friendly attachment, openly stroking one another's legs. These hookups happened all the way along the trail, though I couldn't imagine how they could, given the perpetual stink that pervaded everybody and everything.

Ain't love grand?

Chapter 19: Hoping to meet Diane

I was staying that night at the Sunnybank Inn, known locally—and more colloquially—as Elmer's. It was a beautiful, white Victorian house, perfectly located across the road from the Dollar Store, the thru-hikers' store of choice. For an amazingly reasonable $20, Elmer Hall provided hikers with proper beds in shared rooms, with hot showers in real bathrooms. This was a massive step up from the regular piece of hardboard on which we would normally sling our sleeping gear, as well as the somewhat bizarre assortment of wash rooms we had encountered so far.

I shared with a young guy named Longhorn, from Texas, and we were given the Earl Shaffer room, named after the first recorded thru-hiker. Shaffer did his trip in 1948, aged 29. He caused something of a stir in A.T. circles, because an end-to-end hike of the Appalachian Trail had previously been regarded as impossible. Indeed, A.T. Conference officials presumed that his claim was fraudulent. He used his army rucksack, old, worn boots, and had neither tent nor stove. Extraordinary. No wonder he was referred to as The Crazy One. He compounded this craziness 50 years later by completing the trail again at the age of 79. He must have been quite a man, and I felt privileged to have been allocated his room.

The best features at Elmer's were the all-you-can-eat vegetarian feasts. They were magnificent, only costing an additional few dollars. As you can imagine, A.Y.C.E. was a wildly popular concept for hikers. I'm sure that the Chinese restaurants that offered this on the trail lost a lot of money to hikers when they hit town. Giving a hiker the opportunity to eat endlessly is simply asking for trouble. Offering them unlimited Chinese food is tantamount to commercial suicide.

Hot Springs was well set up for hikers. There was a good, though comparatively expensive, outfitter on the main drag. I bought myself an Appalachian Trail T-shirt that I still wear. The best place to hang out though, on the assumption that you were fed for the day, was the Hiker's Ridge Ministry. They provided free Wi-Fi, use of computers, plus tea and cookies to hikers. They also took a photograph of every hiker passing through, giving us various colored boards on which to paint our names and the date. These were then posted to their Facebook page, open for all to see. There was such a sense of family at the Ministry that I lingered several hours, chatting, drinking tea, and generally hanging out.

Hot Springs had allowed me to reconnect with old friends, and I felt ready to move forward. I knew that I would be running into some of them again, but I was happy to meet and make new friends at the same time.

With my vegetarian breakfast blow-out propelling me forward the following morning, I left Hot Springs behind. My goal for the week was to get to Erwin, Tennessee, where I was hoping to meet up with Diane. While I was certainly looking forward to this reunion, I felt a little regretful about leaving behind my young amigos.

They had been buying into the concept of zero days in a big way, finding the availability of alcohol the very thing to temper the stresses of the trail. They were camped for free, under cover, behind one of the shops in Hot Springs. The zero day easily drifted into a double zero, then, in a few cases, triple zero days. I knew that I needed to be consistent in my hiking; spending the day drinking simply didn't fit into my plans, even though it certainly would have in earlier years.

So, I was alone again and, with my hiking legs well established, I pushed on towards Rich Mountain. The first few miles were fairly comfortable, with easy inclines upwards over about five miles. However, after Tanyard Gap, the mountain seemed to tower in front of me. I started the two-mile climb up and over Rich Mountain. There was a fire tower at the very peak, reached by a side trail that was not on the A.T. Not for the first time, I eschewed this opportunity. Instead, I followed the A.T. down the mountain. While I was aware that these side trails, and resulting views, were there to be savored, I had a quick conversation with myself. I rationalized that the day wasn't very clear and the view wouldn't be that spectacular. My decision was also influenced by the pain in my legs, which were starting to protest vociferously.

Another precipitous dip down to Hurricane Gap, and I was heading back up to Spring Mountain Shelter on another lung-expanding climb. I finished the tough, eleven-mile day at the shelter, grateful for an early night. The weather was deteriorating rapidly, so I quickly ate, then climbed into my quilt no later than 7 o'clock.

By morning, the lousy weather had pretty much run its course, although the whole trail was covered in low cloud that sat ponderously upon me all day as I moved along the path. The lowest point of the day, in terms of altitude, was just under 2,500 feet, with the first three or four miles a steady climb down, punctuated with a couple of sharp climbs to maintain my interest. There was then a tough six-mile stretch that carried me back up over Camp Creek Bald at over 4,700 feet.

These cloudy days with no views coincided with lonely moments, when people were at a premium and the air was thick with contemplation. A dense quiet seemed to descend with the cloud. I always assumed a glumness reserved for those days. I was pushing myself once more, ever-concerned with making up miles when I was able to, so I ignored the first shelter to chalk up a 15-mile day.

As the afternoon progressed, the rain returned, lightly at first, and I relaxed a tad once I was over another bald. The map indicated a gentle slope down to Jerry Cabin Shelter about five miles ahead. As often happened on the trail, believing something to be the case often resulted in a far different outcome, and this day was no different.

White Rock Cliffs and Blackstack Cliffs looked to be no more than part of this easy slope. However, they were difficult to hike, with slippery rocks to cross and close foliage giving a claustrophobic feeling to add to the gloomy clouds. I'd just about had enough of this when I came to a blue blaze on the path. The blaze offered an alternate route to hikers wishing to avoid the exposed ridge in inclement weather. As I mentioned earlier, the rain was intermittent at this point. I decided against what I stupidly saw as a cop-out, and headed up the exposed Big Firescald Knob. The exotically named ridge was a series of literal leaps into the unknown. How some of the smaller hikers accomplished this I could hardly imagine. The whole thing was made spectacularly more difficult as the heavens decided to open a mere 50 yards after I had ignored the blue-blazed, safer, side trail.

I called Diane over FaceTime on my phone. Such an action was rather ill-advised, because she was able to see, in vivid motion pictures, how alone I was, and how little I could see. Putting my phone away, having alarmed my already over-imaginative Puerto Rican, the rain really got into gear. Soon, every rock had turned into a potential pratfall as I hopped from one to another. Several leaps were of three or four feet and, though this wouldn't normally be an issue, I was terrified for about 45 minutes. I negotiated each leap with a silent prayer to somebody whose very existence I'd recently decided against.

Of course, I eventually made it to Jerry Cabin Shelter and sat quietly enjoying the company of others for the first time that day. We were all reflective of another milestone, having passed 300 miles.

I had had a conversation with my brother Mike, a few miles before this. He related the distance as equivalent to going on vacation as a child, with our elder brother, Dave, and our parents. We used to spend an entire day driving across, first, England, and then Wales, on quiet roads. I had hiked pretty much the same distance over mountains. We were both awestruck when we looked at it in that context, and returned to the subject several times at 300-mile intervals throughout the hike.

Having lost most of my younger companions, possibly temporarily, to the wonders of alcohol, I now found myself surrounded by a new group of youngsters with a similarly intoxicating habit. They are more commonly known as stoners these days, but used to be referred to as potheads in my day.

How these guys—they were nearly always guys—fit into what I used to call civilization, I just don't know. However, they embraced everything about trail life with an endearing openness. They would find various wild vegetables along the way, picking edible items with the gusto and knowledge of a true hunter-gatherer. Once at camp, these intrepid adventurers would balance their pots precariously at the edge of campfires. Given their drug of choice, the guys all developed the infamous "munchies" and most maintained, or even increased, their weight on the trail—unlike the rest of us. They would also wallow in the filth of the A.T., and laugh constantly. While I was aware that this laughter was significantly as a result of their smoking habit, I felt that it was more than that. To a man, they were polite, intelligent, happy, and, truthfully, some of the most delightful people I had met. I had found another example of something you find on the trail that you would rarely be exposed to at home. I felt truly privileged to have shared their journey.

It was now the last week of April, with the weather improving all the time. Temperatures were rising as we lurched towards May, and flowers were blooming in the woods. Some of my winter clothes were becoming redundant, but I held onto them in case I had to face another shivering night. The fear I'd felt in the Smokies was something that I wasn't eager to repeat, so I figured that the extra few pounds in my pack were worth the effort to prevent a rerun.

Leaving Jerry Cabin Shelter that morning, I was full of life, getting into my stride, and looking forward to another 15-mile day. I'd been told that you ease into these longer days, and that had certainly been the case for me. I'd made no conscious effort, but was starting to put in the miles I had been expecting at this stage. I was still dubious about the anticipated 20-mile days in Virginia, but I felt very much on course and at ease with myself.

There was a quick reward on this gorgeous day, with another meadow at about 4,700 feet, crossing the wonderfully named Big Butt. I'm not sure what it was about these places, but they hit the spot with me, especially on sunny days when I could walk quietly alone. There was a magic to them that evoked long Sunday afternoons near my childhood home in the U.K. My folks had a house that bordered woods and fields, and I thought nothing of wandering around all day long in those fields. I was sometimes alone, but more usually with a bunch of youngsters until our parents would call out for us to come in. There was never any plan to be within earshot, but we all seemed to drift nearer to home, like migrating salmon, by the time the sun would start its fall in the sky.

My 15-mile day was self-imposed, because I chose to avoid Flint Mountain Shelter and moved on to Hogback Ridge Shelter. I felt that I was on something of a hot streak and didn't want to interrupt my momentum. I breezed past the first shelter, and was rewarded a couple of miles later by a terrific guy providing Trail Magic at Devil Fork Gap. His wife, Jersey Girl, was hiking the trail. He would meet her most nights in his RV, where she would spend the night. Providing Trail Magic was his way of thanking those on the trail who had been friendly to his wife and were helping her to achieve her dream. My calorific intake only lasted a short while, for I had a three-mile climb up 1,500 feet to Frozen Knob, before easing down the other side to my target for the night.

Another uneven camping spot gave me a fairly sleepless night, and I was slow to rise the following morning. I was not normally one of the earliest risers and, in fact, was regularly last to leave camp. Of course, this was apart from the stoners, for whom time was something of an abstract concept. I suspect the truth of the matter was that I tended to dilly dally, and not get into gear, while most of the others were all efficiency, and soon on their way. Normally, leaving late did not play to my advantage. Many times I would arrive at roads where a person, or church, had left a cooler full of goodies, only to find that the cooler had been stripped bare. On those occasions I would loudly curse my tardiness.

On this morning, however, it was my tardiness that worked for me. As I descended into Sam's Gap, just over two  miles into the day, I met a couple of smiling guys, Charlie and Bob. They were putting up a sign to tell hikers of Trail Magic at the gap. They directed me to Patricia, the wife of one of them, and I became their first visitor of the day. Now, if there is one thing that most hikers crave, it is pizza. Not only did they have pizza, but it was still in the heating cover, fresh from the shop. To make it even more of a dream example of this trail wonder, they had local beers—on ice! So, there I was, with a couple of my stoner friends, eating hot pepperoni pizza and glugging back beer, in a chair, on a gloriously sunny day. They even also had fresh fruit. Few days started better on the trail.

Chapter 20: On the way to Erwin

With my pizza, beer, and fruit competing for space in my stomach, I set about the long climb to the magnificent Big Bald. This promised spectacular 360-degree views and, on this gorgeous day, they would erase the memory of the previous day's cloud and gloom. I often found that a spectacular morning, or a sublime sunset, could nullify hours of wet misery.

It was a real battle to make the final push onto the bald itself, yet once I was there, I could see what the fuss was all about. I'd risen to over 5,500 feet and the views had definitely stepped up a gear from what had come before.

Apparently, in the early 1800s, the bald had been inhabited by David Greer, a hermit, described as "cantankerous" in my guide. Quite what he had to be cantankerous about I couldn't fathom. It seems that he was spurned by a woman, though I'd have thought every daybreak must have lifted his heart, with every sunset the perfect nightcap. He clearly didn't buy into the concept of plenty of fish in the sea, because he set up in a small cave-like structure on the top of the bald to eke out his days away from the world in general and women in particular. Apparently, he declared himself sovereign of the mountain at some stage, and, after killing a man, managed to escape justice on grounds of his self-evident insanity. David, or Hog, as he became known, due to his less-than-pristine lifestyle, was eventually shot in the back by a local blacksmith. This was a sad end for an early hippie. Subsequently, Hog's Bald was renamed Big Bald.

Happily, none of this craziness was in evidence on the day I passed over the bald. There were several hikers taking the load off, enjoying the spectacular views and the warmth of the sun.

Longhorn, my roommate at Elmers' in Hot Springs, was there. With him was a crew composed of Hawkeye, whom I had met on my first night at Springer Mountain; Bo, a rather serious-looking young woman; and Science Tooth, a geeky guy with a great trail name. It turned out that I had also met him on my first night on Springer Mountain. Given that I knew three of the four, I decided to join them. I quickly dozed off. Several others came through, while some day hikers came from the opposite direction. All stopped and either talked or dozed; it was like Starbucks but without the coffee and annoying music.

I opened my eyes a short time later, only to be faced with an extraordinarily hairy armpit belonging to a female hiker. While I had already seen less than perfect grooming on the trail, this seemed somehow excessive. I couldn't help but stare for a few seconds, only to be caught by the owner of the hirsute pit. She was lying face up, her jacket temporarily removed, with her hands together behind her head. We locked eyes for a couple of seconds. She followed my gaze downwards and smiled conspiratorially, before shrugging in an expansive gesture, presumably supposed to convey "What's a girl to do?" She was right, of course. Hiking the Appalachian Trail was a tough environment to maintain so-called normal living conditions. We tend to be so tied to conventions in everyday life that coming face to face with something so innocuous—though so strangely shocking to one such as me—I had to reset my preconceived notions of civility and recognize that "What's a girl to do?" was a reasonable response to my rude, inquiring look. I felt like farting out loud to re-establish my hiking bona fides, though, of course, being British, I didn't.

I had intended a longer hike on this lazy day, but the warmth of the sun, the leisurely company, and the views conspired to keep me on Big Bald until my resolve for a longer day weakened. I decided to settle for Bald Mountain Shelter, just a mile farther on.

While I was still largely alone, I felt part of the coterie of hikers on that mountain. I was warmed by not only the sun but also the bond that grows every day between ordinary people doing an extraordinary thing. The hike was a shared experience, with people flitting in and out of our lives and with no competitive animus. We had a common goal that would only be enhanced, not harmed, by others completing their own challenge. The commonality of purpose applied whether they were out for just a few days or going all the way to Katahdin.

At just over 5,000 feet, Bald Mountain Shelter was one of the higher shelters I stayed at, with the elevation contributing to a dramatic drop in temperature overnight. Several of the youngsters chose to return to Big Bald just before sunset and, in hindsight, I wish I had joined them. While I had shared their day, I was never a permanent part of any group during these early miles. I watched, regretfully, when they returned in darkness, rapturous at the sunset. It was entirely my fault not to have embraced the opportunity. They had even asked if I wanted to join them as they left. I'm afraid that my British reserve came into play and I declined. Sometimes, it was difficult to differentiate a stiff upper lip from a pole up my backside.

There were very few spots to pitch a tent near the shelter, so I opted to sleep inside that night. I also ran into the first Brit I had met on the trail. However, she was hiking so quickly that I never saw her again after that night in the shelter. There were plenty of Germans on the trail. Apparently, German television regularly runs a documentary about the A.T., and it is enormously popular in Germany. I often hiked around Germans and was told by one that the documentary had avoided the difficult bits, making the whole hike look like a 2,000-mile stroll in the park. As she said to me, somewhat bitterly, "Zey lies to us." Welcome to the real world.

Sleeping in the shelter always had one significant benefit—I didn't need to pack away my tent. This had been slowing my departures in the morning and, without that constraint the following day, I was able to get on the trail before 8 o'clock. That was still pathetically tardy, but it enabled me to go for the 17-mile trip into Erwin.

I had originally hoped to meet Diane in Erwin. She needed one of her sisters to come and take over care of her parents, so that she could join me. I couldn't stall my hike to wait for them, so we were constantly readjusting our meeting point to coincide with one of the girls getting there on time. Consequently, we had to reschedule this time, and I simply continued my trek north.

With my early start, along with my ambitious day, I motored along. I can't explain why. I just felt more energized than in recent weeks, and my hiking legs swept me along on my way. I spent a large part of the day hiking with a terrific young guy, Little Foot, who had only just turned 18, and his companion, Hat Trick. These young men were hiking at a far faster pace than I was used to, but I never fell off their stride. For me, it was one of those rare times when I got a distinct benefit from hiking with other, faster hikers. I'd previously considered this to be an impediment, often resulting in a fall that would slow me back down to a trudge. For some strange reason, this felt different. I was elated to begin the long climb down into Erwin. I realized that I had moved my mileage up a notch, and that I was getting into the right frame of mind for 20-, or even 25-mile days, in Virginia. I knew these longer hikes were required to make Katahdin by the end of September. The White Mountains in New Hampshire were going to slow me dramatically, so these long days in Virginia were critical to my whole hike.

After an endlessly long switchback downhill into Erwin, during which we could see the Nolichucky River gleaming below us, the first building of note was the famous Uncle Johnny's, a.k.a. the Nolichucky Hostel. The place was slammed, with hikers in various states of undress milling around among backpacks hanging from all available spaces. It was extremely convivial and very full, but I'd decided that a motel was the way forward. Diane had booked me into a local Super 8, a name that rarely, if ever, lived up to expectations.

While hanging out with friends, old and new, I called for a cab. A charming lady took me to the Super 8 after a mini tour of Erwin. She charged me peanuts for the ride, giving me her number in case I needed a cab later. She wasn't going to be available the following morning, so she gave me the number of the town's most well-known resident, Miss Janet.

Miss Janet is something of a trail legend. She fell in love with the trail, and hikers, as a teenager. She spends most of her time providing free lifts, Trail Magic, and just about anything that most hikers need. She embodies the spirit of the trail. I made a mental note to call for her the following day to get a lift back to the trail. I believe that it is never a good idea to bypass a legend.

With a much-needed shower and desperately needed laundry under my belt, I was ready to eat. I met up with several hikers in Azteca Mexican—nachos, burritos, and beer beating out the call of pizza. Others left before me, and I had a last beer by myself before calling my new friend for a lift back to the motel. While I was reflectively sipping my beer, I took a "selfie" that I foolishly sent to my wife.

I had started out the trip as a chunky 245-pounder, and

this picture showed that I was rapidly wasting away. When I weighed myself later that evening, I found that I had lost 37 pounds in just over five weeks. To say that this caused some alarm to Diane would be understating the fervor with which she discussed the picture with me. I knew that it showed I was losing weight fast, and my attempt at humor—"at this rate I should disappear sometime in early August"—was met with no appreciation. She was worried, and I was thoughtless in making light of it. However, I felt well. I'd hiked more than 300 miles and had never been fitter. All she could see was a skeletal figure, albeit a 200-lb skeletal figure.

As if by magic, I was picking up a food drop the following morning in Erwin. Diane had really gone to town. I had asked for three packs of pasta. Diane had sent six. Four Snickers became eight, and so on. When I asked her about it, she told me that she had "thrown in a little extra" because she had seen for some time that I was losing weight. The "little extra" not only filled my bulging food bag but I had to empty out my dry clothes bag to allow for the slack to be taken up. As a consequence, from then on I would hang two bags each night to give the bears additional choice. Very nice of me, I think you'll agree.

Having arrived in Erwin after the post office had closed that Friday evening, I was anxious to collect my package when the office opened at 10 o'clock the following morning. Consequently, I had several hours to kill, and it occurred to me that there couldn't be a better way of killing time than gorging myself on a gargantuan breakfast. Asking around, the local Huddle House was the place to be, so I wandered over to this establishment to set about my task with gusto. It was one of my more memorable breakfasts. I demolished three fried eggs, at least ten rashers of bacon, and a huge slab of hash browns, along with two biscuits and gravy and a gallon of coffee. I was in the process of ordering a couple of bonus slices of French toast when I realized that the post office was open and I should be on my way.

Waddling across the road, I quickly made the executive decision to limit myself to the Curley Maple Shelter that night, only four or five miles up from Erwin. A number of factors influenced this decision. First, I was carrying about five pounds of food inside me. Second, Diane had given me another ten pounds to bulk me up further. Third, the terrain seemed to go straight uphill. Add to that a 10:30 start time, and my limited ambition looked just right.

The start time turned out to be rather optimistic. I called Miss Janet on the chance of cadging a lift back to the trailhead, and she told me that she could pick me up by noon from the Super 8. As I thanked her, she thanked me straight back. Right on time, her battered old van turned up at my motel with several hikers onboard and various destinations in mind. There was the obligatory stop at Dollar General, as well as McDonald's, which was necessary for several guys as they tried to stuff even more calories down their throats.

Nothing was too much trouble for Miss Janet and we went by her daughter's home to pick up a few more vagabonds who had camped on her porch. The trail does this to some people; reasons for their generosity don't actually matter. She didn't ask me for any money, though there was a sign on her dashboard telling the reader that donations for gas were gratefully received. I gave her $15. She even told me that was too much but I insisted. I felt compelled to pay it forward, even though I knew that 15 bucks more than paid for any gas she had used on my behalf. After all, it is the Miss Janets and other less well-known figures who contribute to making a hiker's life on the A.T. more comfortable, so they need to be cherished.

Chapter 21: Out of Erwin

The hike, though short, was tricky and sharply uphill at the end. I finally got to the shelter, puffing and panting. I was happy to be there after about two or three hours. Even better, I met several of my young friends who had eventually made it out of Hot Springs. Naturally, they had caught up with me. The shelter was full and the whole area looked like a tented village. The only downside was that there was no privy on-site, so I knew that the following morning would be a less-than-pleasant experience. The expression "toilet paper minefield" was never more apropos.

A bunch of section hikers from Augusta had shown up, and I knew we'd have a terrific evening. There was a great vibe at the shelter, but I was totally unprepared for the main event.

Several of the youngsters—part of the self-styled group "No parents, no bedtime"—found a challenge written in the shelter. The gist of the challenge was that teams of two had to run back down the mountain; hitch into Erwin; order two large pizzas in the pizza shop; buy 24 cans of beer; then carry their booty back up the mountain in record time. Bloody demented, if you ask me, but, incredibly, we soon had another team—from the "7 a.m. Crew"—wanting to take part. The vintage hikers, including me, looked on in disbelief as these crazy kids, on the stroke of 5 o'clock, hurtled back down the mountain.

We all sat around chatting about the challenge, then realized that our hiker hunger couldn't possibly be put off for about four hours. Pots and pans were soon doing what they do, and turning out pasta, rice, and mashed potatoes by the bucket load. With so many people, space was at a premium, though everybody moved up when asked, and we all ate comfortably. The Augusta hikers had lugged vodka up the mountain, and they generously shared some of their ample supply.

Amazingly, less than three hours after they had careened downhill, the four adventurers returned, cut, bruised, but victorious. With four large pizzas and 48 beers in tow, there was no shortage of volunteers to help them with their haul. We were all suddenly having dinner 2.0.

Those of you reading may well ask what we were going to do with the remnants of this party. I'm pleased to say that the

Augusta guys stepped forward manfully and took away the boxes and the cans. Sometimes, magical stuff happens, and you can only wonder about karma repaying good people.

By now, I would normally have been in my tent, on the way to sleep. But, with so many full hikers and a crackling fire warming us, about 15 of us sat around, jabbering away. Of course, this was the sign for one of the younger guys to produce a joint, take a deep drag, then pass it on. This happened on the other side of the circle to me, and I had time to decide whether or not I was going to partake. I know this isn't a big deal to some people, but it is to me. I have absolutely no issue with anybody wanting to smoke dope; indeed, I've already mentioned the affection with which I held a lot of my stoner friends on the trail. I'm also sure that booze is far more harmful. That said, when you've tried to clean up your act from whichever is your chosen poison, it feels slightly retrograde to dabble, in however small a measure, so I eventually declined.

I've already referred to my relationship with booze over an extended period of time, but this hasn't been my entire experience with drugs.

I've never smoked a cigarette in my life, although I used to take the very occasional, jumbo-sized cigar at the end of a formal dinner. I found it to be an overwhelming exercise, a task to be completed rather than, as I expect is the case for most, savored. I was always exhausted when I finished. Beyond that, booze was my constant companion for so many years. Apart from one very silly moment at the age of 40, when I tried a joint with friends, I had stayed away from drugs entirely.

That all changed when I divorced my second wife. I was suddenly a single man, nearly 50 years old, and more nervous than most people thought I was about being on my own. My first marriage had overlapped with my affair, and subsequent second marriage, so I had been with somebody from the early '70s right through until 2001. Many will recognize this as a mid-life crisis, while others will see it as exactly what happens when an older guy with money comes back on the market.

I presumed that the fact that I was very well paid, owned a spectacular apartment on the River Thames in London, had no children living with me, and was able to articulate entire thoughts in more than one sentence, using words with more than one syllable, probably boosted my case with the female population. I also hoped that having all my own teeth, a mop of slicked-back, silver, politician's hair, and a face that didn't frighten people excessively, may have helped in my search for a partner.

What I hadn't expected was the enthusiasm with which I would be welcomed into this market. I found this to be especially the case with women a lot younger than me, though old enough to know better. I was faced with an age range that stretched down to 30—though once, shamefully, to 22—and up to the mid-50s. I was staggered at not only the availability of women but also the indignities they were prepared to undergo in order to share part of my time. While I don't recommend married men to make this change voluntarily, do not ignore the opportunities that arise should you find yourself waking up on a Sunday morning without anybody warm beside you.

Along with this plethora of women came a culture of drugs, most noticeably in the younger ones. I used to wonder if they needed to take drugs to go out with an older guy.

After the break-up in 2001, I was soon dating Kelly, 19 years my junior and working as my receptionist. To be fair, it isn't as if I'm claiming any originality here; I checked off all the usual stereotypes. We were together for about nine or ten months, though she remained living at home. We tended to spend the weekends and the occasional evening at my apartment. I knew that she was a social cocaine user, and I was reticent at first, but eventually inquisitive as to what the attraction was. We were due to have dinner one evening in London. She came to me in the late afternoon, armed with a smile and a small amount of cocaine.

Once I'm ready to do something, I quickly become impatient at delays. I suggested we should have some prior to leaving my flat. This amused her, and I found myself very much in the junior role in our relationship, for the first and, as it turned out, the last time.

Kelly expertly, to my eye, prepared the powder for consumption and lined it up neatly on the kitchen countertop. With all the wide-eyed excitement of a kid at Disney, I bent down with my rolled banknote. I snorted as vigorously as possible, sending the powder deep into my system. Nothing happened. Kelly told me to be patient as we walked to the nearby Italian restaurant. A glass of Barolo and a plate of beef carpaccio did nothing to blunt my disappointment. I told Kelly that I was less than enthusiastic about her pastime. She laughed and said, "You're talking about ten times faster and five times louder than normal. It's working just fine." I did feel very clear in my head, but simply replied that I'd like another hit when I got back home.

That evening, returning to my flat, we tried for a second time. While I can't say that I felt like a million dollars, I certainly had a strange experience. I sat on a bar stool, in the kitchen, holding Kelly at the waist. She rested her head on my shoulder. I was talking quietly—at least I thought it was quietly—to her. It was a very chilled experience, and entirely contrary to what I understood would happen. Suddenly, it was 6 a.m., and the sun was peeking above the horizon to the east. We were exhausted, crashed into bed, falling asleep instantly for about six or seven hours. We woke in the afternoon and dragged our heads for the rest of the day. My initial impression of cocaine was that it gave me two days in one, then took one of them back the very next day.

Other women took cocaine or smoked dope, sometimes both, and I would adapt my habits to theirs while the cast of characters circulated through my life.

Chloe was never a girlfriend in the biblical sense, but she became my date once for a trip, with wives and girlfriends, to a tennis tournament at Queen's Club in London. I had been invited by an old friend in a business capacity, so I took my boss's secretary along. She was fun, gorgeous, blond, about 20 years younger than me, and single. She also gave me one of the best lines I've ever heard from a woman in those far-off single days.

The tennis was something of a sideshow at these events, because we were royally entertained in a marquee. We never needed to leave our seats, for we were plied with a constant stream of food and booze. Chloe suggested a break outside in the sunshine. We walked out and sat at a picnic table with just two chairs.

"I've got some coke, do you want some?" she asked, after we'd chatted about nothing for a couple of minutes. "Why not?" I replied. At this point, she gave me the line I'll never forget. "Lick your finger and put it between my legs." I should add, by the way, that an alternative method of ingesting coke is to rub it on your gums. That worked better for me than the ubiquitous snort.

I looked at Chloe with an idiot grin, slowly sticking my finger in my mouth, before withdrawing it slowly. Call me old-fashioned, but that works so much better when a woman does it. As instructed, I moved my hand under the table to find the coke in a small packet on her lap. The fine powder clung to my wet finger, which I then withdrew. As nonchalantly as I could, I put it up to my mouth, and slipped it in as if I was pondering one of the great mysteries of the universe, slowly rubbing the powder across my gums.

Even though nobody was paying attention, I couldn't help but feel that there were searchlights upon us, and a band was playing film noir music in the background. Of course, we weren't spotted. Now that we had lit the blue touch paper, we sat back, and waited for the fireworks to begin. It was extraordinary. Within a minute, I felt like the King of the Universe. My friends will tell you that isn't too much of a step for me, because, until I moved to America, I always acted very much that way all my life.

My vision improved, with a cutting clarity, as if aided by the finest lenses known to man. Magnificent thoughts rushed through my mind, each more brilliant than the last. My movements were faster, but, I thought, more graceful. I also had an almost explosive need to get away. I wanted to get Chloe into a private place, and share my brilliance with her, along with several bodily fluids. I shook my head, in a vain attempt to clear it, then made my excuses to leave. We were soon on our way. As before, time accelerated, and, in what seemed like five minutes, we were back at my flat. This was normally a 45-minute cab ride on a good day, so the effect of the coke was wearing off by the time we got in.

Suddenly, the closeness and certainty of imminent sex had worn off. I was with Chloe, my boss's secretary, not my lover. I then did what, for me at the time, was an unusual thing: I gave her an out. I told her that, should she stay, I was going to begin to undress her. I also said that, should she go, I would have no hard feelings, which was somewhat ironic given the circumstances. Chloe made the eminently sensible decision to go home, and I kept a friend instead of finding a future ex-girlfriend. Those were far tougher to find, and nowhere near as disposable.

While not all of those thoughts were rushing through my mind that evening as the joint was passed around, you can probably see why I was reluctant to take even a drag of a joint while on the trail. I loved those who did it, and enjoyed them while they were high; I was just not in the frame of mind to join them. To a degree, this left me once more on the periphery, but it was a position with which I became increasingly comfortable as the months went by.

Chapter 22: Meeting Diane

I had to plan my mileage about three or four days in advance. Whether it was to make sure that I was in a certain town at a certain date for a package from home, or to make a meeting point when friends came to meet me, careful forward planning was critical. Knowing when post offices were open could affect your mileage for a day, and could even strand you in a hell hole for a weekend.

As a consequence, most nights were spent tucked up in my quilt, with the Kindle app on my iPad showing the *Appalachian Trail Thru-Hikers' Companion*, and planning the next few days. I'd started out with the paper copy of the guide, tearing out pages as I passed through. Eventually, I found out that I could get a copy specifically for the iPad, so I sent the book home, minus several pages, and loaded the guide onto the tablet.

I knew that Diane had booked a flight to get her to North Carolina at about lunchtime in three days' time. That meant that when I left Curly Maple Shelter the following morning, I had 31 miles to cover in the next two and a half days. We were planning to meet up at Carvers Gap, which was a high gap at about 5,500 feet. Experienced hikers, or even marginally experienced hikers, will immediately notice that this was a dumb idea. However, I'll return to that later.

In the interim, my plans for the next few days were a 13-mile hike to Cherry Gap Shelter, followed the next day by just nine miles to Clyde Smith Shelter. The last day was going to be another nine miles up and over Roan Mountain (see how easily my inexperience slips off my tongue), then down to Carvers Gap, where I would be reunited with my love. What could possibly go wrong?

Now that I had got into my stride, 13 miles was no real challenge, so I enjoyed the hike on a gorgeous, sunny day. I even treated myself to a leisurely lunch at the aptly named Beauty Spot, another magnificent field at the top of a mountain.

I can clearly recall making a short video of my surroundings, luxuriating in the sun as I ate my regular wrap with mayo and salami. I was alone and happy to be so, waving at a couple of day hikers as they passed through, though not really engaging them. I was in my own space, it filled me with joy, and

I didn't want to share it with anybody. At night, I'd re-engage with others, but days were mine. Despite being an extremely gregarious person in my usual habitat, it was fine by me if I didn't see or speak to a soul all day. My only real explanation for this is that nature somehow filled the gap caused by an absence of people. That may seem a little trite, but it was certainly how it felt to me on that day.

With my lunch contentedly taken, a few simple falls and rises led me to the slightly intimidating, yet magnificent, Unaka Mountain. I found it to be a bit of a mission to climb, but so rewarding at the top. Unlike my preferred balds, this mountain was covered in a deep, dark, tall forest of spruce. Even with the sun high and bright in the sky, under this natural canopy the darkness descended as if in a fairy tale. I half expected Red Riding Hood to pop her head round the corner of one of these dark trees. Following the white blazes was always an important element of hiking the A.T., though the path would normally suggest itself without these painted directions. On Unaka, the blazes were critical. I found myself paying rapt attention lest I strayed off deeper into the woods.

On the way down the mountain, now out of the spruce forest, the weather started to turn. Rain was clearly in my future. By the time I got to Cherry Gap Shelter the decision as to whether or not to tent had long been made. I was sharing with the mice and filth for the night because I didn't want to pack a wet tent in the morning.

Against the odds, no rain came, though there was a lousy forecast for most of the rest of the week. For this reason, along with my need to ease up on my mileage, I pushed on to Clyde Smith Shelter. It was a straightforward hike, so I ended my day just after 1 o'clock. Several people came to the shelter for a break, then hiked on to the next one, while I settled down to read my Kindle in the watery sunshine.

The weather developed quickly, with clouds rushing in, followed by copious amounts of rainfall, thunder, and lightning. Of course, people were no longer moving on, so the shelter rapidly filled up. We soon discovered the truism that location is everything. Blue, one of my fragrant tobacco friends, discovered a leak in the roof right above his head. After some rapid temporary repairs, during which he re-directed the dripping water to the back of the shelter, he settled into some semblance of comfort. Typically, he was undeterred by this unfortunate turn of events.

Happily, the rain subsided just before sundown. Jandle, an affable New Zealander, set about building a fire that warmed and dried us all. This was the biggest fire I saw on the entire trail, made even more impressive when taking the limited choice of available, dry firewood into account. The lull in the storm turned out to be temporary. We all rushed back into the shelter when the sky burst, immediately dousing our fire. This time, there was no let up, and we were battered throughout the night. I was lucky to remain completely dry, while poor Blue had to constantly shift and rearrange his temporary handiwork throughout the night. In the morning, he brushed it off. "Just another day on the trail," he laughed, while he packed up after breakfast looking like a hairy George Clooney in *The Perfect Storm*.

I made it out of the shelter earlier than most that day. I took the opportunity to gamble that a break in the clouds meant that the rain was over for a few hours. I had only nine miles to cover prior to meeting Diane, but I was aware that I'd have to cross over the top of Roan Mountain. That would take me above 6,000 feet, and the trail would be wet and likely slow me down. I was lucky for the first couple of hours. Then, just as I was starting the four-mile climb, the rain returned. This downpour was endless, with the trail growing into a lively stream for a much of the time.

Appalachian Trail Clubs in various regions along the entire trail take responsibility for maintenance of their local sections. The maintainers construct water bars, which are diagonal trenches across the trail, backed up by logs and rocks. As the water streams down the trail it hits these water bars and is carried off to the side. The process normally works really well, yet the sheer amount of water sometimes overwhelms those efforts.

This day, the rainwater was far too much for the water bars to cope with, and I was slogging uphill through a stream, slowing my pace dramatically. The four miles took me about three and a half hours. I was grateful for a short break in Roan High Knob Shelter, just after the summit and the highest shelter on the trail. The building was one of very few enclosed structures on the trail, doubtless due to its altitude. There were two floors, and the place was full to overflowing. Many of my young friends from previous miles were there, having decided to spend a zero day out of the bad weather. It was gratifying to be greeted so warmly by them. I was always amazed at the youngsters' capacity to spend a zero day, or two, then hike over 30 miles the following day with no apparent effort.

As soon as I ventured inside the enclosed walls, I realized why they were zeroing. The place was full of smoke, mainly fragrant, as people were lounging about, many still in their sleeping bags. Once again, a twinge of regret made an appearance, though I knew that partaking in their fun wouldn't work for me. I had a quick lunch, chatted with those around me, and headed down to meet Diane. Everything was going to plan. And then, it didn't.

A sad truth about life in this early part of the twenty-first century has been the extraordinary reliance some of us place on mobile phone technology. I am as bad as anybody in relying upon this tiny device to keep me in touch with the world. This had never been more clear than when I'd completed my relatively easy downhill hike to Carvers Gap. I was devastated when I saw "no service" on the phone where my AT&T bars were supposed to be.

Diane should have landed at 12:30 p.m., about 40 miles away. By the time she had left the airport, hired a car, and driven to meet me, I thought it would be between 2:30 and 3 p.m. I was there soon after 2 o'clock, and it was only then that I realized that we had a problem. The trail emerged from the trees into what the Brits used to call a "pea-souper." This was a fog so thick that I could hardly see more than 30 yards in either direction. The day was also bitterly cold, and I had stopped hiking, so my temperature began its natural downward spiral.

I couldn't go anywhere, I couldn't contact her, and, by extension, she couldn't contact me. Even if she was in the vicinity, I wouldn't have been able to see her and, as I'd pulled all my clothes on, my body temperature was only going in one direction. This certainly wasn't my happiest moment on the trail.

Suddenly, a couple of cars turned up and I hoped that one of them contained Diane. It turned out to be a bunch of hardy ladies out to test themselves against the elements on a day hike. I was looking about as pathetic as an old guy can look, so they asked me if there was anything wrong. When I explained my dilemma, one offered me her Verizon phone—which had a solitary bar—and I tried to contact Diane, without success. Defeated, I glumly told them that I'd just have to stay put and hope she turned up eventually.

I must have ratcheted up my pathetic appearance, because the goodwill that permeated this trail came to the fore once more. One of the ladies said that she would be happy to leave her car unlocked, and that I could wait inside. Apparently, my English accent and tragic figure marked me out as somebody to be trusted with a $40,000 SUV. I gratefully accepted and sat there, out of the cold until another car drew up.

Convinced that it was Diane, I got out quickly, but it turned out to be an elderly couple, who offered to take me down the mountain to try to get a signal or to make a call from the park office. I locked up the SUV and, as arranged, placed the keys on top of one of the front wheels, then gratefully accepted the offer. Ten miles later, still unable to reach Diane, the good-hearted couple returned me to the top at my request. I also discovered that Carvers Gap was covered in low, thick cloud and not fog.

It seems that Diane must have turned up there when I left. However, after being spooked by the cloud, the mountains, the roads, the lack of any human activity, and the fact that I was nowhere to be seen, she made the sensible decision to get to our hotel, an hour away in Boone, North Carolina, in the hope that I would contact her there. Having AT&T, she also had no service at the top.

Of course, I knew none of this at the time, so I was really in a jam. The ladies had abandoned their hike, returning to their car, and left me. I started to march around in an attempt to warm myself, and this worked fairly well. Eventually, after another hour at the top, a young student and her boyfriend appeared. The two of them had been tracking red squirrels for the park service. They offered to run me down to Roan Mountain, a nearby village at the very bottom of the mountain. I threw everything into the back of their car and relaxed, knowing that all would soon be well. I was worrying for Diane though, because I knew that she would be traumatized by this.

At Roan Mountain, I thanked my new friends when they dropped me off at Bob's Dairyland, a local family restaurant. My spirits lifted when I saw a couple of old friends, Stylze and True Story, eating outside. In my hurry to call Diane, and share my story with my friends, I pulled out my pack, but left my trekking poles in the car. Unfortunately, I didn't realize this for a good 15 minutes, but, by then, the students had disappeared.

Eventually, I got a line and spoke with Diane. She was in a dreadful state, crying relentlessly, and just too upset to be able to come and get me. I didn't want to put her through anything else, so I got a lift from a local hostel to Boone. I got there at 8 o'clock, nearly six hours after we were supposed to have met.

I had very few terrible days on the trail, but this probably topped the list. It brought home to me both my limitations, and the fragility of our communications, when we rely on phones to help us out.

Chapter 23: A tourist in NC

I'm sure that I had changed—although I can't speak to that—but I knew immediately that Diane had altered since we had been apart.

After our initial delight in seeing each other, and our mutual reassurances that we were both fine, we decided to treat the next couple of days as if we were on a weekend break together. Boone was a college town, with trendy restaurants and plenty of stuff to see nearby. We ate brunch, we had dinner, we visited touristy places, and we strolled hand-in-hand around small villages. All the time, I could tell that Diane was watching me, worried about how skinny I had become. She was also concerned about the various cuts and bruises I had sustained. We were together, but not back in sync with one another.

I was watching her as well.

Diane comes from a large Puerto Rican family that loves and cares for its own with a devotion and fierceness that is a wonder to see for this rather disconnected Brit. I first met her folks, in Orlando, at Thanksgiving in 2006. As we drove away from their home, Diane said, "My mom is going mad." This sounded like a throwaway line at the time, but it turned out to be a precursor to her mother's developing dementia, then Alzheimer's disease. My parents died relatively young, so I never had to see anybody go through this debilitating disease, but from what I have seen in the past nine years, I'm glad that this never happened to them.

Her mother deteriorated over the years, and, by 2011, Diane was driving from our home on the Gulf Coast to Orlando about twice a week. This was a 250-mile day for her and incredibly wearing. Also, it impacted her ability to spend sufficient time in helping develop our insurance agency. Eventually, we decided to sell the agency to allow me to plan my hike.

We bought a new home in the same area, in December 2012, in preparation for her folks moving in with us. We expected it would be another two or three years before we would need to make that decision. Two months later, they were with us. Over a period of 24 hours, a few weeks prior to this, both were hospitalized. Diane basically lived at the hospital in

Orlando for three weeks, while I was back at home, 120 miles away.

I don't think I was aware how ill they were at that time. Diane would give me updates over the phone, but I certainly wasn't prepared for the day when two ambulances turned up at my door, with one in-law in each ambulance. They were wheeled in on stretchers, both on oxygen. I remember thinking, "This is real, and this is what our lives are going to be dominated by for the next few years." Our lives were put on hold at that moment.

Living with her folks had many problems, but Diane faced them all with a selfless equanimity that astounded me. She was a fearless advocate for them, making their lives as comfortable as possible, while giving no thought to her own health or well-being. She was also fortunate to have a bunch of supportive sisters who tried as best they could to visit and help her whenever possible. However, they had their own lives, and lived elsewhere, so Diane had by far the brunt of the responsibility. It is a testament to her that her mother and father started to prosper physically, all the while deteriorating mentally.

Their confusion, especially her mother's confusion, could be heartbreaking. We'd be watching TV, with the volume turned down low, when her mother would appear in our peripheral vision. Diane would leap off the sofa to comfort her. Her mother was often lost and, when Diane got to her, she wouldn't know where she was. Diane would carefully turn her round and show her "Mama's Room," printed on the door. "Papi's Room" was across from her room, with their bathroom in between. To see somebody's brain turn to mush before your eyes is both a shock and an education.

The sheer presence of her folks in our lives eventually convinced Diane that they needed to be in a facility that could allow them some freedom while providing them with care. Thus began the truly harrowing process of finding a new home for them. I wish I could tell you that the options were great, but I'm afraid that, unless you have a fortune to spend, assisted living facilities wouldn't be the first choice for your nearest and dearest. That isn't to say that the staff didn't try within the limitations of their resources. More, it is that a congregation of old people, with serious mental and physical challenges, is hardly a convivial bunch to be around. It seemed to me that, whichever location was chosen, Diane's folks would begin their inevitable decline when surrounded by death and decay.

How wrong was I?

Eventually, the leading facility was vetted, then chosen, with my mother-in-law the first to move. She was put in the memory-care wing, a *One-Flew-Over-The-Cuckoo's-Nest* place if ever there was one. It was horrendous. After just one or two nights, Diane decided that her mother wasn't as far gone as the other residents, so she moved her mother into a "regular" unit. She also moved my father-in-law in at the same time, so they started their new life, still believing that they were living with us.

In those early days, Diane would go back and forth at least once a day. The fact that they weren't with us permanently helped us to have some down time together. Her sisters would come and take over from time to time, allowing us to have the odd break at the beach or, once, a trip to New York.

By the time we met again, five or six weeks after I set out from Springer Mountain, Diane was fully engaged with her parents, spending several hours twice a day with them in their facility. The fact that I was having my adventure probably didn't ease her stress too much. I always felt that she bought into my project far easier than she would have done had her folks not been taking up so much of her time. With me away, there were no longer limitations on how much time she could spend with them, and those added tensions showed in her face.

In much the same way that I was still hiking, she was still caring for her folks. While the two of us tried to re-engage over those two days, something had shifted. There wasn't time to find out what had happened, so we both tried to enjoy ourselves as much as possible, hoping that all would be well when the hike was over.

Despite this little hiccup, she was still the person I wanted to be with, and even that surprised me. In times past, I had always shut down relationships that weren't working, moving from one to another with alarming speed, with more overlap than was probably healthy, or fair. But, with Diane, I never considered shutting down or moving on. They say that the third time's a charm over here, and I've always hoped that this would remain true for me.

Our time together was short and bittersweet, with another parting looming over us, so we became tourists. We also looked for a few things to help me on my way. Of course, my trekking poles were top of my list, so I made the schoolboy error of going cheap, finding a $20 pair at Walmart. I've found in life that if something is cheap, then there is always an excellent reason for the cheapness. In this case, it turned out that my poles had a predilection for collapsing at critical moments. Unfortunately, I didn't find this out until I was back on the trail and using them the following day. I also bought a new bandana, having left the previous one in a shelter. I got a blue one, to solidify my Mighty Blue credentials once more.

Diane was eager to fill me up with unlimited quantities of food. This was an issue that I took on as more of a challenge than a problem, and ate with no guilt.

I wanted her to see what I had been doing, for she was never going to get on the trail with me. I thought the best way would be to show her the mountains from a safe distance. We drove to Blowing Rock, a small park that has spectacular views, and where we could both see the magnificence of the mountains I'd been inhabiting. To be frank, I was impressed myself when I was able to look from afar. When I was hiking, in the green tunnel, it was sometimes difficult to visualize the altitude at which I was walking. Seeing those mountains gave me a perspective I hadn't imagined. I couldn't say what Diane was thinking, but she gamely went with it. She continued to support me as she had done for the past 40-odd days, and would continue to do so until my hike had run its course.

I already knew that returning to Carvers Gap, at over 5,000 feet, was not going to be an option for Diane. I worked out that the best way to get there—as well as the best way for Diane to get back to the airport—was for her to drop me at the Mountain Harbour Hostel. This was the hostel that had delivered me to her a few nights before, so I called ahead, and established that they would complete the process by getting me back up to the gap.

Mountain Harbour Hostel was famous on the trail for its extraordinary breakfast, a veritable calorie-fest that promised much, and fully delivered. It turned out to be the best $12 I had spent on the trail to this point, giving me the calorific intake to walk 100 miles, though only 15 were needed that day. With my leisurely breakfast filling my stomach, we were late getting underway, but by then the clouds had lifted. I could see the mountaintops ahead, and I knew that it was going to be a beautiful day. I also knew that I'd be starting again. I'd be making new friends while trailing my old friends, but I was alive to the challenge. Invigorated by seeing my lovely wife, I got out of the shuttle, tightened my straps, took one last look at the hated Carvers Gap, then headed north.

Chapter 24: Back on the trail

I had been keeping a blog of my journey, and reading a few of the comments that came in. When my post taking me to Carvers Gap had been uploaded, I soon got a note from a reader. She told me that north of Carvers Gap was some of her favorite hiking in the south, with balds, already my favorite feature, in abundance. So it proved, though the start was a little truncated. There was a temporary, detoured switchback around the first few balds, apparently to control erosion of the path. However, there was soon plenty to see, for the path eventually moved up to the top of the magnificent ridge.

There is something other-worldly about hiking on balds, particularly when you have spent days on end in the forest. You can see the path sweeping ahead of you as you take in your surroundings, luxuriating in the fresh air, the sunshine, and your own vitality. My breakfast was powering me along and the hike itself wasn't overly demanding in those first five or six miles. I allowed myself a lunch stop at Overmountain Shelter, probably the largest shelter on the trail. It was a red, converted barn that had once been used as the backdrop for the movie *Winter People*. When I arrived, the place was deserted, so I took full advantage of the best privy on the trail. The privy was open to the sunshine and facing an unimpeded view across the meadows in the distance. There were rarely times when I enjoyed using a privy on the trail, but this was one such occasion.

A few weeks later, a hiker told me that he had stayed overnight in the shelter and that the two-storied building had had an unnerving effect upon him. He became fixated upon a mouse scratching around 20 feet above his face. Somewhat inevitably, the mouse fell. The hiker, stunned into immobility, could only watch in mounting horror as the poor mouse plunged in apparent slow motion, appearing to grow exponentially in size with each foot fallen. The mouse landed on his chest and scampered away. The poor guy claimed never to have slept in a shelter since.

With my huge breakfast now deposited into history, in a manner of speaking, it was time to eat. I replenished my calories with a wrap—mayo and salami—before moving on.

I was ready to tackle two beautiful balds. The first was the pleasingly named Little Hump Mountain and second was Hump Mountain. These became Little Hump and Big Hump to me. Climbing these two marvelous balds gave me one of the most exhilarating afternoons of my hike, with the whipping wind keeping the temperature at comfortable levels and the sun always beaming down. I had read about the balds in many of the books I'd used in preparation for my trip. None came close to the sense of solitude, beauty, and downright majesty of these features.

They were covered in dense, native grasses, with a narrow path snaking through them. Near the top, rocky outcrops allowed the hiker to sit, rest, and enjoy the views, especially back to Roan Mountain in the near distance. I've since looked at photos and videos that do absolutely no justice to the tremendous effort required to get to the top. That was very much the case with Big Hump, which appeared to be close, but felt as if it was ever climbing further into the distance.

There was temporary relief descending from Little Hump, as I dropped below the wind at Bradley Gap to gather strength for my assault on its big brother. My hiking was so strong that day that I couldn't wait to get at it again. I pushed on, actually shouting with excitement. While I had my fair share of grim, quiet, and, frankly, miserable hiking days, when I was really flying—when I was in the zone—I would often roar out of pure joy at what I was doing. Those days were great.

Unfortunately, my Walmart poles weren't so great.

Looking back, I'm sure that I chose the $20 Walmart poles because I was with Diane, and I knew that my expenses had been racking up. Had I been by myself, I would have certainly bought a straight replacement set of my Black Diamond poles, so accustomed had I become to them. To be fair to Diane, she would never have suggested buying the cheaper pair; I just felt that I needed to show that I was aware of my spiraling bill from the hike.

I had learned that reliability was key with poles. I often had to put my entire weight on them leaping down from rocks, so the chances that my Walmart replacements were going to do the job for me were somewhat less than slim. And so it proved. During what was otherwise a day of unrestrained joy, my poles collapsed on me three times. Fortunately, none of the collapses resulted in a fall, yet I became wary of trusting them after the first time they gave way. As a consequence, I slowed towards the end of the day.

I moved lower in elevation and through Doll Flats, the North Carolina-Tennessee border. I was in my third state.

The five-mile, nearly 3,000-foot descent from Hump Mountain left me tired but satisfied with my day's exertions. There was an additional bonus, in that US19E, the road at the bottom of the mountain, lay less than a third of a mile from the Mountain Harbour Hostel. It was an easy decision to return, given that I knew a repeat of breakfast would work well the following morning. With such a short distance to cover, I soon found myself tented and comfortable in a field at the back of the hostel. I was chatting amiably with a couple of guys: Belch, who I often saw later on the hike, and Lover Boy. There was also a very attractive, rather ethereal, middle-aged woman hiking south. She claimed to have been hiking since November. She was a bit unsettling, though less for her attractiveness than for her strange demeanor.

Lover Boy had injured himself a few days prior, and had been hoping that he would recover sufficiently to get back on the trail. However, by this point, he had resolved that his hike was over. He was waiting for a relative to arrive and take him home. As luck would have it, I noticed that he had exactly the same poles as the ones that I had lost a few days before. I suggested that I could get his poles to Katahdin, even if he couldn't get there. I offered him $50. My offer appealed to him, so a deal was struck. I was safe once more. I always felt an obligation to try and take those poles to their destination but, in the way of these things, it wasn't meant to be.

After my great day over the Humps, I was far less ambitious on the following day, a Saturday. I wanted not only to go on another calorie frenzy but also to listen to my Mighty Blues play the last match of their regular season. They were in contention for a playoff spot, so my focus would have been elsewhere had I started hiking straight after breakfast. Consequently, in a soporific, post-pancake stupor, I set up outside the main house. I was just about in range of the patchy Wi-Fi and listened as my team scraped into the playoffs.

My sporting itch duly scratched, I set out at midday with the Mountaineer Falls Shelter in my sights. I had a modest nine-mile target over far easier terrain, passing the gorgeous Mountaineer Falls on the way. I'm not sure what it was, but I had an extremely uneasy feeling when I got to the shelter. After ten minutes sitting around, in an eerie silence and waiting for company, I decided to move on. I was hoping to find an occupied tent site, because I knew the next shelter was a farther nine miles away and I wouldn't be able to get there before nightfall. My guide showed an official tenting area only half a mile after the shelter, with a water source. I presumed that I'd find other hikers there. To be honest, I was mortified when I got there to find nobody had stopped. I was at Camp Fuzzy Legs—not an entirely encouraging name. As the sun dipped in the west, I accepted that another barrier was about to come down. I'd be camping alone for the first time on the trail.

I decided that my routine shouldn't change. I set up my stove, had an entire packet of mashed potatoes, refilled my water bottle, then climbed nervously into my tent as the sun fizzled out. I've since reflected—and it certainly sustained me that night—that I got an irrational feeling of safety when I zipped into my tent. There was only the thickness of the tent walls between me and the outside. I know it makes no sense, but it always felt that way. The bug net would keep out anything crawling and the tent wall would prevent larger interlopers. Exactly how bears might view this I couldn't guess, yet I never felt threatened, despite hearing a few sounds most nights. I fell asleep, only to be woken at about midnight by feverish, though playful, screams somewhere further up the hill. I cinched my quilt ever-tighter and hunkered down, eventually falling back into a deep sleep.

I was very pleased with myself the following morning, having crossed another barrier. The routine remained, and I contentedly boiled water for my coffee and oatmeal before heading out.

I was now comfortable at the prospect of days hiking between 15 and 20 miles. I had passed 400 miles the previous day and, while it would have been nice to share some of the hike with people, I was aware that I was currently outside of a bubble. Bubbles formed as groups of hikers merged and stayed within several miles of one another, getting together at shelters. I had come adrift of the bubble in front of me, while the one behind hadn't caught up with me. My sedate pace would soon sort that out.

I had been planning on a 16-mile day, all the way to Laurel Fork Shelter, but ended the day a couple of miles short of the target. I gave in to the temptation to go and see the charming Bob Peoples at the "rustic" Kincora Hiking Hostel. Bob suggested a $5 donation and ran a very relaxed shelter. There was a bunk room, well water—so much better than tap water that you wouldn't even think it was the same stuff—a kitchen, showers, and real toilets. Despite these riches, I chose to tent again. I spent the evening chatting on the porch with Bob and his lugubrious helper, Lumpy, along with several new faces— Walkabout, Hard Hat, and Vista.

I also met Chuck, as yet otherwise unnamed. He had quit his job the previous day and decided on a whim to hike the trail, without telling his girlfriend of 14 years. He was hideously unprepared and, at 340 pounds and just over seven feet tall, he was certain to stand out. This would have been especially so if he used the loaded gun that he was carrying. He even had a porta-potty, intending to pack out his waste. As a very dear friend of mine would say, "I can't see that catching on."

Meeting Bob Peoples was one of those moments when I knew I was in the presence of a good man. He does so much work on behalf of the hiking community, including trail maintenance. His hostel welcomed one and all with a simple suggestion of a tiny donation. All hikers were made to feel part of his extended family. I felt privileged to have met him.

With my Nalgene bottle and water bladder full of delicious well water, I set out for Hampton early the following morning. I was considering a swim at the bottom of Laurel Fork Falls, just a mile into the day. That would only happen if I could work up the nerve to brave the temperature and the current. The previous day, I'd dangled my feet in a stream and the water had felt absolutely freezing, so I didn't anticipate much of a dip. More seriously, a father and his son had died in 2012 in the undertow of the falls, so I was a little cautious.

I was feeling lonely on this sunny day as I entered Laurel Fork Gorge. The path slowed me as I took my time getting to the spectacular falls. Once there, I decided to hang out for a while with my feet in the water, a safe distance from the falls themselves. People came by and sat around with me while we watched the water crashing down, before they all moved on. I reasoned with myself that I'd most probably never be coming this way again so, after some internal deliberation, I stripped down to my swimming shorts and waded in.

In an attempt to capture this ridiculous idea for posterity, I set up my camera phone on its tripod and turned the video on, confidently turning to wade into the water, leap under the water, then return quickly to dry myself. That was the plan, although it didn't quite turn out that way.

My wife told me later that the funniest video I shot on the entire trail was this one. I had made the critical error of leaving my camp shoes by my pack so, barefoot, I tried to pick my way through the devastatingly slick rocks to get to the deeper water nearer the bottom of the falls. Bearing an alarming resemblance to a crazed orangutan, I ultimately slipped and fell on my backside in about 12 inches of water. I looked utterly ridiculous. Somewhat chastened, I returned just as slowly, and reset the camera before repeating the process. On this occasion, I wore my camp shoes to help negotiate the rocks. I wish I could tell you that it was much better, but that would be a lie. I eventually reached a sufficient depth in which to swim, so I splashed around for about 30 seconds, then returned to dry land before my body turned blue and my heart stopped beating.

Drying off in the sun, I checked the guide to see that my target for the day, Hampton, was less than eight miles away. The trail would cross the Laurel River several times, via bridges, then take me up and over Pond Mountain Flats. There was a 1,700-

foot switchbacked climb and descent so, now dry, I set off once more. There was a welcome break at the top, as the Pond Mountain Flats lived up to its name for about half a mile, with a level stroll that gave my legs some relief. Switchbacks sent me down the other side to US321, about three miles from Hampton. This climb down, however, was not without incident.

As I left the gorgeous falls, I realized that I hadn't fallen for a couple of weeks. With seven as my total to that point, I was foolishly hoping that perhaps my tumbles were over for the trip. Much like the commentator's curse, I immediately fell on my backside, trying to negotiate a tricky tree root. That was okay, though worse was to come.

On the way down, after the relief of Pond Flats, I lost my footing, falling forward. With the weight of my pack pushing me even further forward, I landed flat on my face. Despite my weight loss, I was still over 200 pounds, and a 200-pound man doesn't fall lightly, especially going downhill. I was stunned and even thought that I might have knocked myself out for a few seconds as I lay there, recovering. By some distance, this was my most painful fall to date. Once I had composed myself, I had to pull out my first aid pack to clean and try to dress the resulting cuts on my hands and legs. I also had a small bruise on my cheek.

I'm afraid that this fall, more than any other, punctured much of the confidence I had built up to this stage. I even asked myself the inevitable question, *What the fuck are you doing out here?* It was, of course, rhetorical, and I let the thought hang in the air, pulling myself to my feet and slowly continuing down the mountain.

I didn't fancy hiking into Hampton, so I stuck out my thumb, more in hope than expectation. Within minutes, a friendly young man stopped his truck, told me to sling my pack in the back and to climb in. It was my first hitch, and I immediately spotted something that became a trend going forward. As I climbed into the truck, I noticed, smiling to myself, that the young guy wound the window down. Smelly hikers, while normally courteous, do nothing to enhance the ambiance inside a small cab. Outside air tends to restore the balance somewhat.

Chapter 25: Hampton to Damascus

Hampton was a pivotal town for me. I met somebody who helped me look at the remainder of my hike in such a way as to make sense of what I needed to do in order to achieve my goal.

I chose to get a private room in the Braemar Castle Hostel. The building was an imposing stone edifice that looked as if it had been plucked out of Scotland and deposited in Tennessee. I loved the place, feeling immediately at home in my private room—a steal at $25. The alternative was to share in the bunk rooms downstairs for $15. There were clean showers, a full kitchen, and a living area that was quiet and provided passable Wi-Fi.

A young lad was acting as a kind of janitor-in-residence. We sat in the living area chatting about the trail and my progress so far. He gave me an obvious tip, although it was one I hadn't considered. I used that tip for the remainder of my time on the trail. I had told him that I was hoping to get back home by the end of September, and that my mileage had crept up recently, so I was fairly confident I was going to make it in time. He said, "You should work out how many miles you have left to cover, divide that by the number of days until the date you want to be home, then use that number as your target for the day." I did the sum, coming up with my number, which turned out to be 12.3 miles per day.

He continued. "Using that number, give yourself credits for everything more than 12.3 miles, and debits for everything less. That way, you can earn zero days when you've accumulated enough credits." This made complete sense to me, and, from that day forward, I would look at every day's mileage as something to be considered with these credits in mind. My confidence was also bolstered, because the target was less than I was doing by this time, even though I knew my daily mileage would slip when I reached New England. Veteran hikers would say "of course" when I shared what to me was a revelation. Others were as impressed as I was; some even used it for the rest of their hike.

You're welcome.

The town itself was disappointing for those of us wishing to satisfy our urge for a decent burger. I made my way across to Brown's Grocery—owned by the Braemar Castle Hostel owners—and ordered an unappetizing frozen burger. The place doubled-up as the local laundry, so I set about doing that as well. Whiling away the time, waiting for my laundry to finish, I heard an English accent. I introduced myself to Trigger, a guy from the U.K., who had teamed up with Shellback, an American.

I had been in the United States for nine years by now, and it was only on this trip that I discovered that I no longer tuned in to the American accent. However, I did notice British accents when I heard them. This surprised me, but I suppose it is part of the process of integrating into a new country. Another link in my chain back to the U.K. was broken.

These were men in their 40s, and we chatted for a while as Shellback studiously worked out his provisions for the coming week. He was a quiet, diligent man, with a great sense of humor, constantly providing riddles in shelters to drive hikers crazy. Most hikers wrote short messages in the trail logs found in all shelters; Shellback provided us with something to think about.

Trigger complained that choosing his own trail name hadn't worked out as he had hoped. Most Americans presumed it was something to do with guns or Roy Rogers' horse. I immediately knew that he had named himself after a much-loved character in a British comedy series on TV, *Only Fools and Horses*. It was good to speak with a fellow Brit, reminiscing over a culture we both grew up with, all the while aware that I was growing further from that culture.

The three of us fancied a beer, though Tennessee's odd drinking laws prevented us from getting just the one. We eventually persuaded the proprietor of the store to run us to a gas station, where we were able to buy, I believe, a dozen beers each. I had two, then left the balance in the fridge back at Braemar Castle. My guess is that my janitor friend stayed in Hampton for the constant supply of free beer that he was able to accumulate from thirsty hikers. Not a bad gig if you can get it.

With a 12.3 mile baseline very much in my mind, I was able to grab a lift back to the trail the following morning. I started the day with a pretty three-mile hike around Watauga Lake, a gorgeous view that was constantly visible through the trees on a warm, sweaty day. Emerging from the forest at the north end of the Watauga Dam, I crossed the dam. Then, there was a long climb up from about 1,700 feet to about 4,000 feet over a sustained period, spread over about ten miles.

It turned hotter than I had experienced so far. Even at the elevated levels, the temperature was in the low 80s, so I was having something of a sweat-fest. This meant that I was constantly looking for a water source at which to slake my thirst. I got through at least seven or eight liters that day, perhaps as many as ten. I can't recall a time during which I sweated more profusely, or for such a protracted period of time, as I did in those three days out of Hampton, into Damascus.

More worryingly, I had noticed for the first time that the downhills were taking their toll. After the long hike down from Pond Flats—just before Hampton, and where I had fallen badly—my knee had started to grumble at me. More than ever, I became aware of how fragile each hiker's attempt was, and how it was luck that avoided a trip-ending injury far more than fitness or even determination. Just feeling the twinge in my knee was enough to make me worry.

I was happy to eventually make Iron Mountain Shelter after 15.7 miles. I was even happier to have 3.4 miles of early credit in my bank. You probably can't relate to this unless you're a hiker, but such small things can seem like huge victories when you are in the woods. Every night, with much ceremony and some swelling of the chest, I'd happily record my credits for the day. On the other hand, if I had underperformed for the day, I'd feel a bit down as I subtracted from my overall total. These small things enhanced life's pleasures, becoming big things in their own right.

I seemed to have become part of another bubble while I was in Hampton. There was a very friendly atmosphere at the shelter, with many new faces to meet. I'd already noticed that the relationships I was building on this hike were very temporary. They could be quickly established, with everybody understanding the ephemeral nature of these interactions. The easiest way to instigate a conversation was to ask about trail names. That often led to a back-and-forth that shifted easily on to more general topics. I had many, far deeper, more intimate discussions that started as a response to "So, Mighty Blue, what's with the name?"

I also reflected that shelters were wonderfully leveling places, because we all knew that we'd hiked the same distance, so we all knew the pains and difficulties we'd been through to have reached that precise point on the trail. A mutual respect was earned, and people were comfortable to interact as equals in this environment.

Resolved once more to add credits, I set out for Abingdon Gap Shelter, nearly 17 miles away. I'd be passing on a shelter after only about eight miles, so I felt that my new calculation was positively influencing my hiking. The terrain was also comparatively benign, with no significant climbs to negotiate through the day. Once more, it was very hot. I soon became thirsty, so you can imagine my delight when I followed a short path down to Tennessee 91, and spotted a cooler next to a tree, out of sight from the road.

This happened regularly in the south, with many hikers still on the trail. Churches, hiking associations, and individuals would come to roads and leave these coolers on the path packed with goodies for hikers to pick through. The sight alone would always make me salivate, contemplating that moment of opening. I was hoping for Coke, Gatorade, or water to drink, and Snickers, Cliff bars, or the ubiquitous peanut butter to eat. The signs were good, as a clear message on top of the cooler instructed "Stop here for a drink and a snack." Since these were activities for which I was eminently qualified, I dropped my poles, bent down and opened the box as if I were examining King Tut's tomb.

Do you recall that feeling when you were a kid, at Christmas, and you wanted the latest toy on the market, but you knew that your parents couldn't afford it? You hoped against hope that they'd been able to get it. On the big day, you unwrapped your present full of anticipation and irrational hope, only to find some duct tape and a bottle of hydrogen peroxide? Well, no, that didn't happen to me at Christmas either, yet that is exactly what I got when I opened the cooler. I can hardly express to you how gutted I was. I howled "Noooooooo" out loud. Another late start had got me to the cooler after my fellow hikers had taken their share, leaving none for me. Curses. I really needed to get on the road earlier.

Once again, a disproportionate disappointment came over me and I skulked on to cross the road. I was temporarily, and totally unreasonably, pissed off at the world.

Fortunately, I then happened upon what I described in a video at the time as the most beautiful spot I'd found on the trail to that point. The road led up and over a stile, through a farm, across cattle fields, and towards a bench, one of very few on the entire trail. Never one to miss the opportunity to sit in some modicum of comfort, I took the load off and contemplated the glorious scene that unfolded in front of me.

Sweeping hills brushed the horizon, busy birds flew and chattered around me, and the lush grass at my feet dared me to stay pissed off. To my eye, the location was very English in nature, which may be why I was so drawn to the spot. It was also from an England of my past, possibly with my parents and brothers when we were younger. Whatever it was, the place was magical. I quickly cheered up, and laughed at myself over the empty cooler, restoring some equilibrium.

It was rare that I couldn't shake a mood just by looking around me during that summer. If you want to know what that feels like, I strongly suggest jumping on to the Appalachian Trail somewhere in Tennessee and going for a walk. For that matter, jump onto the trail anywhere; you'll rarely be disappointed.

Once again, you're welcome.

The rest of that day's hike—as if a counterpoint to my disappointment with the depleted cooler—was another new high in terms of my own hiking prowess and enjoyment. I still had about 11 miles to go to Abingdon Gap Shelter, but I just tore it up. I moved comfortably and well within myself, although without seeing another soul. A last drop down to the shelter, in a lightly wooded area, and I was back among smelly, welcoming hikers once more. It was great to see them.

That evening, over a very convivial dinner, I foolishly got into a conversation about gun control that I should have avoided. There was a very nice old guy, aged 72, who was giving us all the benefit of the Fox News playbook on the issue. I kept quiet for as long as I could. But, when he stated that the Colorado movie shooting could have been immediately stopped by a shooter in the cinema audience, I'd had enough.

It was clear that all of us at the shelter were left of center on this. I felt that a counter-view was called for. I shouldn't have done it. The discussion got a touch heated, much to my consternation, because I remembered that he was hiking the A.T. to work out some anger issues. I'm afraid I got a bit English on him, and bitterly regretted it all the next day, on my walk into Damascus. Happily, we spoke when we saw each other in town, and we resumed as friends. As I thought to myself, *when somebody is talking like a jerk, it's probably best to go and find somebody else to listen to.* My guess is that he was thinking precisely the same thing.

I have already referred to my complete inability to leave camp in a timely fashion. However, with the Virginia state line and Damascus beckoning the following day, I resolved to do something about it that night. Consequently, prior to my run for the border, I decided to set my alarm for 5:45 a.m., and get an early start.

The alarm woke me, and I immediately deflated my sleeping pad to ensure that I wouldn't drop back to sleep. To my entirely unreasonable irritation, I heard activity already going on outside. Once I'd wrestled with my pack and stuffed what I could into it, I emerged to find that three or four people had already left, with others about to follow. I couldn't believe it, but still felt that I had a shot at not being last. I noticed a few more hikers emerging from their tents while I had breakfast. I don't know how it happened, but, quite suddenly, I was alone, wishing "happy trails" to the second-from-last person to be on their way. I eventually left, two hours after my alarm, and I couldn't tell you what I did in those two hours apart from packing and having breakfast. As I trudged moodily away from the shelter, I thought, *Maybe I'll get up at* 4 o'clock *tomorrow.*

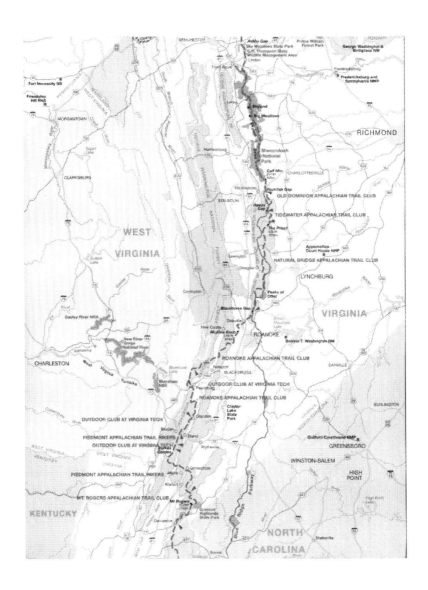

Chapter 26: Damascus to Coolgreen

Damascus is apparently known as Trail Town U.S.A. and referred to in my guidebook as the "friendliest town on the Trail." It is home to the legendary Trail Days, a frenetic annual get-together of 20,000 unwashed people in a town of less than 1,000. I planned to be nowhere near Damascus when the latest iteration took place, about a week after I left. I later heard stories of copious amounts of boozing, vomit, and toilet difficulties. When hikers refer to toilet difficulties in a bad way, it must have been spectacularly unpleasant.

Aficionados of the Appalachian Trail seem to love Trail Days, and I'm sure it was great for all the reasons I would have found it unmissable in a past life. But three days of emptying my stomach from various orifices was not on my schedule if I was going to keep to my target. I also felt that camping in the town for that extended period of time would have required something of a restart. I feared that I'd take several more days to get back up to speed.

With that said, Damascus certainly welcomed hikers, and hikers certainly felt at home. As I wandered through the short main street, in the only clothes that I wasn't washing, I got used to some bizarre sights. For me, town gear, when washing clothes, involved a rather natty combination of my water shoes, my swimming shorts, and a T-shirt I got from Hot Springs. Normally, I wouldn't be seen dead on the streets of a town in such an ensemble, but it looked just fine in Damascus. Walking around like that, you would think that I'd be loath to criticize others for their dress sense. However, one German guy insisted upon simply wearing the tightest Speedos around town. With the best will in the world, even if you have the world's greatest body—and he didn't—Speedos just never work.

I treated myself to a private room at the Hiker's Inn, a laid-back place that charged me just $45. They also took my laundry away, returning a clean version to me the following morning for the bargain sum of $5. I took advantage of the free time by reading on the front porch, rocking away, and was totally content for a couple of hours.

A quick meal at Dot's Inn Cafe with Trigger and Shellback, the guys I had met in Hampton, and I was ready for bed.

I was expecting to put in another 15- or 16-mile day on leaving Damascus, even though the forecast threatened rain at some point. Unfortunately, my plans went somewhat awry when the promised rain started after about five miles. I leapt into action in the time-honored fashion. My waterproof pack cover was in a convenient position for quick retrieval. I pulled off my pack and reached inside for the cover, only to realize that it must have slipped out back on the trail. This was not exactly what I was hoping for. A few minutes later I was hoping for it even less, as the rain progressed to a downpour of epic proportions.

Fortunately for me, this discovery happened right by a road, so I stuck out my thumb in the hope of cadging a lift back into Damascus. I can only imagine how appealing I must have looked at this point, with water cascading from every part of my body. The number of cars that stopped was a predictable zero. After about 15 minutes of grinning like a demented prison escapee, slanting my thumb jauntily to one and all, a young couple emerged from the woods. They offered me a ride when they made the fatal error of asking me what I was doing there.

So, about three hours after I'd left Damascus, I was back. I had to shell out $40 for another waterproof cover and another $15 to take me back to resume my hike. I was on my way again, dryer but poorer.

My day was now slightly truncated, leaving me back at the road several hours after I had left it. Saunders Shelter was my only realistic destination. With my 12.3 miles-a-day target firmly in my brain, it would also result in an almost three-mile debit on my total. I considered going further, and perhaps camping by myself, but, by the time I got to the empty shelter, I was ready to stop. The rain had been intense all day, with the prospect of more later. I thought that if I was going to be by myself, I might as well set up my tent inside the shelter to stay dry. I'd then at least have a shot of avoiding the attentions of the cute, furry occupants.

Suddenly, there was a rush for the shelter. While several people set up outside, I felt increasingly uncomfortable—and a bit daft—having a tent inside the shelter. Still, nobody insisted that I should act like an adult, so I spent the night both dry and inside my tent, with no interaction with rodents of any kind.

I was also delighted to be joined by 19-year-old Simba, one of the fearless young women on the trail. I hadn't seen her for a while. She had been doing plenty of zeroes, as well as plenty of 30-mile days. Such a combination was so alien to me that I simply shook my head in disbelief. Simba was totally comfortable hiking by herself, though at this stage, she was with a couple of guys and another girl. Her fearlessness constantly amazed and troubled me. While the trail was generally safe, there was always the possibility of running into somebody who had bad intent. These concerns would return not only much later on my hike but also the very next day.

In the morning, I made it out of camp fairly quickly, for me. I set off, intent on getting my mileage back on track. It would have helped somewhat if I'd taken the correct turning out of the shelter for, about 20 minutes later while I was hiking at a good pace, I heard the voices of my previous night's companions only about 50 yards away. I'd walked a loop and was back within spitting distance of the shelter. Sometimes, simply shaking your head at your own stupidity is enough comment, though if I'd been able to kick myself in the ass, I would have certainly done so.

I was heading for VA600, just shy of a 15 mile day. The trail took me up and over Whitetop Mountain, at over 5,000 feet, the second highest peak in Virginia. While I was at the top, I worked out that I had about three miles to go to the road crossing. Here, I was hoping to be met by Ron Roberts who, along with his lovely wife Phyllis, owned the excellent Coolgreen Bed and Breakfast. I called Ron, and told him where I was, as well as my expected journey time down the mountain. I made good progress, getting there about ten minutes before him. Rain had threatened the whole day and certainly looked to be falling in the distance in virtually every direction. Luckily, I had managed to avoid it all day long.

While I was waiting by the road, the indefatigable Simba emerged through the trees, bristling with energy and vitality, as always. By now, it was nearly 6 o'clock, with the sun falling in the sky. She told me that she was going to either camp by the road or push on, in the impending darkness, to Thomas Knob Shelter, over four miles ahead. That was worrying. For a moment, I considered asking her to come to Coolgreen with me. However fearless these young women were, I sometimes thought that they felt immune from the violence and evil endemic in everyday life. The prospect of a pretty young woman, pitching a tent beside a remote road, gave me pause. The alternative—going another four miles in the dark—wasn't much more appealing.

On the other hand, of course, I'm afraid my reticence stemmed from the fact that I was a 61-year-old married man. Taking a 19-year-old with me to a B&B wasn't realistic, whatever my motivation. I know it is ridiculous, and she certainly wasn't my responsibility, but I felt a little conflicted as Ron drew up. I bade farewell to Simba, telling her to stay safe. She always wrote a message in the shelter logs, so I was very relieved when I read one such message a few days later.

Coolgreen was a delight. Built in the early years of the twentieth century, it was the fully restored home of L.C. Hassinger, of Hassinger Lumber, Konnarock, Virginia. The house was also once the Iron Mountain Lutheran School for Boys and Young Men. In America, it was regarded as an old house, so Ron and Phyllis clearly took great pride in not only their home but also their hospitality. The house was set in a tranquil, rural setting, with views of both Whitetop and the upcoming Mount Rogers.

They offered a full breakfast but, probably because I had perfected my hungry pathetic-loser look, Phyllis included me in their evening meal. She was a terrific cook and, even though I had had no expectation of dinner, I ate at least half of the delicious food on offer. Phyllis was of the just-in-case-ten-other-people-turn-up variety of cook. Home cooking even beat burgers, so you can imagine how grateful I was. After dinner,

Ron took my dirty washing, returning it to me the following morning while I was polishing off another hearty breakfast.

He was hilarious, constantly throwing out one-liners, often aimed harmlessly in Phyllis' direction. He gently teased her about pretty much everything. It was great to be an observer of a married couple who didn't take themselves too seriously, and were confident enough in their own relationship to playfully rib one another. I felt more at home than I had done thus far on the trail.

When breakfast was over, Ron dropped me off in the same spot that he'd picked me up, though not before he'd taken me on a detour to find an ATM. By a considerable distance, this had been my best stay to this point. My concerns about Simba notwithstanding, I set out that day with a lighter heart and a real skip in my step, which is not easy when you weigh over 200 pounds.

Chapter 27: Coolgreen to Marion

That Sunday morning was misty to start with, but it soon burned off for another sparkling day. Early on, I was hiking behind a family of three, and the first mile or so took us up and through some pretty meadows. I was about 40 yards behind them when we all heard the sound of an unhappy bull. I couldn't describe what that sounds like; just believe me that you'll know it if you ever hear it. When we'd entered the field, there was no sign of any livestock. As I heard the sound, I looked up on the low ridge just above me to see a large black bull move menacingly towards the family. Just off to the right of the trail, in the woods, I spotted a bunch of cattle by themselves. The bull clearly didn't take kindly to anybody positioning themselves between him and his harem, so he put down his head and charged.

I was frozen to the spot, too shocked to do anything other than watch it unfold. The ground shook, and the thud of his charging hooves filled the air. Fortunately, the mother in the family had the presence of mind to blow the whistle around her neck. The bull veered away at the very last moment, careening into the woods. Danger averted, we all continued as if nothing significant had happened, although the bull watched us with his girls while we walked on and into the woods further down the path.

We hadn't known there were cows when we entered the field, but the evidence of their presence was before us back in the forest. The path looked as if the herd used it for their own personal bathroom. Plotting a course through piles of poop was at least a change from rocks and roots.

After the encounter with the bull, I was eager to move on to embrace this perfect day. I knew that the Grayson Highlands were coming up, and was excited by the prospect. First, I had to get past Mount Rogers, Virginia's highest peak at 5,729 feet.

Coming out of the forest and climbing ever higher, the terrain grew increasingly rugged. With nothing to block the view, mountains stacked endlessly behind one another into the distance. The trail was wider than normal at this point, although intermittent, large rocks in our path were regular hazards that needed careful attention.

Hikers were spared the need to summit Mount Rogers. There was a half-mile detour to the west that would have taken us to the summit. As far as I was concerned, I was going where the trail took me, not taking short excursions out of my way. I left that to some of the youngsters, who could comfortably go a couple of miles in a completely different direction, hang about for a while on a rock, then return to the trail, and still knock off 25 or even 30 trail miles during the same day. Such activity exhausted me even to think about it.

At Thomas Knob Shelter—which was close to the highest point on the A.T. in Virginia—I chatted with hikers who were trying to work out Shellback's latest riddle. I wanted to stop for lunch at a rock that I'd noticed about 200 yards further on. The rock looked to be bathed in sun, and perfect for a picnic, so I moved on after about ten minutes.

Before I got there, I ran into a bunch of wild ponies that seemed entirely unconcerned about a smelly hiker, allowing me to pet them. I suspect their acquiescence was rather more an attempt to get scraps of food from me than anything else. These ponies clearly didn't know that hikers don't give away food, so they lucked out, with me at least. They were residents of Grayson Highlands State Park, a spectacular combination of rugged mountains and enchanting meadows that combine to challenge the hiker while feeding the soul. It is a very popular, and accessible, part of the trail, with thousands of visitors through the year, many gaining access via a mountain road.

I reached and climbed up onto my rock, setting everything down to enjoy the sun and the views. Below me, the path sloped to a flat area of about half a mile, with more ponies scattered around. The trail then rose once more to Rhododendron Gap and Wilburn Ridge beyond. A commotion in the distance suggested that a hiker's dog had caused a bit of a stir with a couple of the ponies, but the place was otherwise silent. I enjoyed my salami wrap, luxuriating in the sun.

I still had about ten miles to cover before I reached Old Orchard Shelter, so I reluctantly left my lunch perch to move on. The terrain didn't look especially challenging, with gradual slopes for the rest of the day. However, the descent was now formed almost entirely of huge boulders. I slowed considerably. Fortunately, after a couple of miles of this crawl, the path cleared quite a bit and I made camp by about 6:30 that evening.

A bunch of us created our own little tented village in a beautifully sunny clearing. We sat around the fire preparing food or, in my case, boiling a pot of water. I then lobbed in four portions of dried instant potatoes, added a few bacon bits, a smidge of Locatelli cheese, and had a meal fit for a king or, in my case, a greedy hog.

My day in the Grayson Highlands had been a blast, and I sat in my tent that night, thumbing through my guide to see what was in store for me the following day. There were gradual rises and falls, with an early dip down 500 feet, followed by a 1,000-foot climb, then down 1,500 feet, then up 1,000 feet, and down another 1,500 feet. This was like a gigantic roller coaster that you walked instead of rode.

It would have been another great day had I not suffered something of a headwear fail. I wore my bandana over my head, but left my poor old neck to sizzle and fry in the sun. That I had also neglected to apply the SPF 50 proved to be another big fail. I finished the day looking as if somebody had tried unsuccessfully to sever my head at the back of my neck with a blunt knife. It was not a good look.

The sun exposure had the additional effect of exhausting me, so I settled on a 14-mile day—for a 1.7 mile credit—by 3 o'clock. There was nobody else at the shelter. I set up my tent, sat in the shade, pulled out my iPad, and had a quiet read for an hour or so until others started to trickle in.

I was glad that I'd picked my spot already, because we soon had another minor tented village. Eventually, there were a dozen tents within close proximity of one another. That would have been absolutely fine if only I hadn't been situated next to a German guy and his wife. I was deeply asleep when, at 4 o'clock the next morning, his alarm woke me and several of my neighbors. I was miffed at his lack of camp etiquette. When I mentioned it later to another German guy, he said, somewhat enigmatically I thought, "He is East German," as if that explained everything. Maybe the Berlin Wall coming down wasn't exactly the unifier that we had hoped it would be.

My German neighbor compounded his 4 o'clock alarm call by clumping around the camp as if everybody was awake. Of course, several of us were by then. Still seething with righteous indignation (though it doesn't take too much for a Brit to get righteously indignant over the actions of a German), I couldn't fall back to sleep. After an irritated 20 minutes I decided to get up, for others were now on the move. With the sun barely on the horizon, I emerged from the woods into a buttercup-strewn meadow. The early start set up what turned out to be my longest day so far on the trail.

I was heading for Chatfield Shelter—nearly 18 miles away—but I planned to stop at the fabled Partnership Shelter. Apparently, you could order pizza and get a shower, neither of which I intended to pass up. In fact, my eagerness to get there was such that I knocked out the ten miles to Partnership in just over four hours. That's when things slowed down.

Stripping off, I took a shower at the back of the shelter. I then left my sweaty clothes to dry in the sun, while I sauntered down to the visitors center to order pizza. I was told that it would take an hour to be delivered. However, when you are waiting for a 16" deluxe pizza, with extra chili, nothing is going to stop you from waiting. I managed all but three small slices. Having spent three hours at the shelter, I set off with a full tummy and sweat-baked clothes, with renewed energy to get to my destination.

The days were drawing out, so by the time I got to Chatfield Shelter, it was 7 o'clock, but still light. As I headed down the blue-blazed path to the shelter, I noticed that the place appeared to be deserted. I could hardly believe it, and so approached warily. About 30 yards from the hut, I heard a guy call out, "Don't come any closer." He told me he was sick, and that I shouldn't come in. He added that others had passed recently, but had gone on to find a camping spot further along the trail. I asked if I could call anybody, but he simply said that he'd either live or he'd die. This pretty much seemed to cover all the options. There was nothing I could do that he wanted, so I moved on, somewhat reluctantly.

I wasn't going to mention this, because he may have gone for option two, but I did find out his fate once I'd left the trail. Through the magic that is social media, I discovered that his name was Hoba. He eventually had to be taken from the shelter by paramedics. I have no idea what was ailing him, but he apparently recovered and is now fine.

Shaken by this encounter, I now started to worry that I'd be camping alone again. Such an outcome appeared more likely by the minute, for I passed a small opening in the trees that somehow held three tents, but with room for no more. The sun was now dropping rapidly, and the forest was getting more dense. My pace accelerated to something of a gallop as I hurtled along, desperate to find anywhere to camp, or anybody to camp with. Facing the prospect of another night alone, all my insecurities resurfaced. For experienced hikers, this is nothing new, but, to me, it was a challenge. One minute, I was expecting to be chowing down with friendly hobos; the next, I was moving like a charging bull, frantically looking around for somewhere safe to pitch my tent.

It was almost 8 o'clock, with the sun dipping just beyond the horizon, when I joyously emerged from the forest at VA615. All my fears disappeared in an instant, because I knew that I could camp just off the path, on a soft patch of grass. Even more joyous was the fact that the Settlers Museum was located right next to the road. Although it was closed, the museum welcomed hikers at all hours. Trying the door, I entered to find a cooler, with bottles of water and some fruit. I can't recall enjoying an apple and a slug of water so much in my entire life. Once more, the truth that it's the little things that matter the most was brought home to me.

I set up my tent on the lush grass and spent the minutes before sleep thinking about the day. Despite spending three hours at the Partnership Shelter, I'd completed almost 20 miles, mostly thanks to an early start, precipitated by my German neighbor. I had worked hard, both up and down mountains, adding to my hiking strength. My positivity notwithstanding, I was disturbed by the panic that had overwhelmed me towards the end of the day. I thought about the poor guy in the shelter— alone, sick, and with nobody to help him. I was grateful that I'd found my spot, yet my glaring inexperience had unnerved me again. I started to doubt myself once more.

Looking back, with the luxury of time to reflect, I can entirely understand my concerns that night. I think, however, I was probably underestimating how well I had been coping by this stage, and how much I had achieved with no experience to guide me. I recall somebody giving me some advice around this time. He said that I'd gone from doing no hiking at all, to probably more hiking than 95 percent of all Americans. That realization sustained me through self-doubt that would surface every now and then.

You may have noticed that I haven't made too many references to wildlife I met on the trail. The simple answer to that is that there had been so few sightings that recording them would be something of an exercise in futility. Meeting animals, of whatever description, was one of the things that had concerned me at the outset. However, I'd come to the conclusion that, while there were plenty of critters about, none of them were especially keen on making my acquaintance. That was fine by me.

My squirrel record by now was, almost unbelievably, only six. The last of these had been over 300 miles previously, in the Smokies. I'd seen several mice, mainly at shelters, two deer, no bears, two black snakes, along with the charging bull, several cattle, and the ponies. I also saw a lavishly decorated tortoise, which looked as if a three-year-old had been given license with a paintbrush and a bucket of yellow paint.

My no-bears total was starting to irk me. Most of the people I ran into had bear stories to share. Early in the hike—still back in Georgia—I thought I'd seen the rear end of something big as it disappeared into the trees. I couldn't in all honesty mark it as a sighting. I'd just have to wait, but, when it did happen, it was electrifying.

I was ready for another resupply from Diane. I had arranged with her to send my next food parcel to Marion, one of the larger towns that I would visit on the trail. I only had a short, flat, couple of miles to the road the following morning, having booked a shuttle service to take me into town, ten miles to the west.

With the majority of the day to kill in this quiet place after I had picked up my delivery, I took the opportunity to get my laundry done. I then caught up on my blog, and managed to squeeze in a Mexican meal, washed down with a couple of beers, before getting to bed before 9 o'clock. I saw no other hikers, either in the motel or at the restaurant, so the day was a bit tedious, though necessary. I was more than ready to push on early the following morning. My next stop was going to be Pearisburg, about 90 miles further north on the trail. It turned out to be a pivotal spot that helped determine the outcome of my adventure.

Chapter 28: Marion to Pearisburg

An early cab the following morning saw me back on the trail by 7:30 a.m., where I was greeted with dark clouds and the threat of rain in the near future.

The past few days had been lonely for me. I prepared for even more solitude, because many hikers were making their way back for Trail Days in Damascus. Several had arranged lifts to whisk them away, only to return them to the same spot two or three days later. As I said previously, I didn't want to be there for a variety of reasons. However, my credit and debit system was now taking hold in my mind, so I mainly didn't want a bunch of debits to eradicate all the credits I had accumulated in the past week or so. With 90 miles to cover in about six days, that credit would keep increasing, getting me closer to my goal.

I tried to push on quickly to take advantage of the dry start, but the rain came within an hour or so, remaining steady until lunchtime. I trudged gloomily up a slight incline on Gullion Mountain. With the rain temporarily on hold, I stopped for a quick lunch, hoping that I'd be able to get to Knot Maul Branch Shelter without further interruption. Of course, within minutes of my restart, the heavens opened. What had earlier been a steady downpour became an absolute deluge.

I was in full waterproof gear, with about six miles to hike, so a couple of truths about waterproof gear soon made themselves evident. The first one was that hiking with full clothing is a hot business, so the sweat immediately starts to flow. Subsequently, I found myself assaulted by liquid both inside and outside my suit. The second truth was that, however hard I tried to avoid it, I eventually discovered that the rain started to seep in. At this point, I realized that "waterproof" is a temporary condition, lasting for about 20 minutes at a maximum.

The cumulative effect of this mixture of sweat and rainfall was that I had a cold, wet feeling that started at my neck. Slowly, but inexorably, it worked its way down through, and past, my pants, to my legs, then settled damply in my boots. It was grim, and I was very grateful when I reached the shelter. That is, I would have been grateful had I been able to get inside.

The shelter was completely full. Several hikers had seen the weather that morning and had simply hung out there all day. This was not very good etiquette in the hikers' honor system, even though there was nothing I could do about it. Certainly, nobody seemed eager to move anywhere. To add insult to injury, one couple had a huge dog with them. The dog was the size of a baby horse, taking up space clearly meant for a human, though his owners showed no interest in moving him to accommodate me.

There was nowhere to pitch my tent, so I sat forlornly on the edge of the shelter, trying to look as pathetic as possible. This was eminently doable in my case; indeed, it was a look I had perfected. Despite my best efforts in this regard, there were no offers to squeeze me in, so I eventually trudged off. I was soaked to the skin, and had no idea where to spend the night. My insecurities floated, unbidden, into my brain once more.

Only about two tenths of a mile later, I saw a small clearing, with a completely drenched tent shivering by itself in the woods. To be frank, I didn't know what to do, so I just hovered under a tree to try to escape the watery onslaught. After about ten minutes of standing motionless, like a soggy Boo Radley behind the door, my temperature spiraled dramatically. I ventured out from under the inadequate branches, and set up my tent in record time. I heaved in my sleeping pad, bag, and liner, along with my few extras, then left the pack outside under the waterproof cover. This turned out to be the best thing I could have done, because I was back in my cocoon, engulfed in my sleeping bag, and warming by the second. After a few desultory words with my unseen companion—who sounded as jaded as me—I read for a while, and then slept. I was not looking forward to what the morning would bring.

The rain gave up at about three in the morning, stopping so suddenly that the lack of sound woke me up. Where before there had been a torrent, there was silence, broken only by individual raindrops blown from the trees and hitting my tent. There was some condensation inside, but it wasn't too bad. I was happy to be warm and dry for the moment. I knew that my clothes were all soaked and that they would still be soaked when I emerged in a few hours' time. There was nothing I could do about it, so I turned over and fell deeply asleep once more.

As day broke, I stirred, groaned, and immediately deflated my sleeping pad. This had become my default method of getting myself out of bed and into the day. I had slept in black long johns and a matching vest, so they were warm and dry. Rummaging around in my pack, I managed to find my dryish swimming shorts, and pulled those over the long johns to complete my snappy outfit. I looked like Superman after he's been exposed to Kryptonite, following a particularly heavy night on the town. It was neither a good look, nor a good feeling, yet I'd weathered the storm and survived intact. I always tried to take positives out of negative experiences, however dire the circumstances. I didn't realize at the time that I'd be tested again very soon.

Outside, resplendent in my new ensemble, I chatted with my previously unseen neighbor over breakfast. We commiserated with one another over our wet clothes, but we both knew that there was no alternative other than to shove everything into our packs and get moving.

An early lung-burster up and over Lynn Camp Mountain prepared me for what I knew would be the main event of the day: a 2,000-foot rise over five miles that took me through and out of the forest up to Chestnut Ridge, ending at Chestnut Knob Shelter. It made for only a nine-mile day, but I really had to dry my clothes. I hoped that, should the rain stay away, I'd be able to hang a line and get my increasingly shabby and damp garments to dry in the breeze at the top.

What I hadn't expected was the beauty of the climb, especially when I emerged from the trees onto Chestnut Ridge. A long, extended meadow rose constantly ahead of me. While it was tough, the 20-mile views compensated tremendously. I reveled in the day, singing loudly to myself the whole time.

At the shelter, I ran into a number of fellow hikers, including the voluble Racewalker. He was a friendly, older guy, who chatted animatedly when engaged on a subject, but who would otherwise stay silent, and listen to others, or busy himself with his pack.

While dry, the weather was still fairly threatening, so I thought I'd take advantage of the intermittent sun and copious amounts of wind to dry out my soggy belongings. I set up a clothesline between a couple of trees. Not having any pegs, I threaded the sleeves of shirts and the legs of pants onto the line to encourage them to stay put. The socks had to perch on the line, so, with every big gust, I had to field the flying socks like a dog chasing a stick. It was exhausting; I don't know how dogs do it. While I was in sock-retrieving mode, I also set up my tent to dry it out, ever aware of the approaching clouds and rain.

Due to the elevation and consequent exposure to the elements, the shelter had four walls and a door—something of a rarity on the trail. There were plexiglass windows to lighten the place, with individual bunk platforms that allowed a modicum of separation between smelly hikers. Outside, there was a privy and a recent campfire. There was also a line of trees with a 50-yard gap for a spectacular view to the valley below. The valley is known as Burke's Garden, though it is more poetically known as "God's Thumbprint." This name was well-deserved, thanks to a dramatic curve making a horseshoe-shaped ridge that encircled the "thumbprint." It was a beautiful sight.

My drying strategy worked reasonably well, though I had to truncate the effort when the inevitable rain arrived. I gathered everything and scrambled indoors. My socks and underpants hadn't dried properly so, in the dead of night, I reached for them, slowly pulling them on to dry out from my body heat. While this was excruciatingly unpleasant at the time, waking in dry socks and underpants was another minor triumph for me. You've got to take these triumphs when you can get them on the Appalachian Trail.

What I hadn't realized, when looking over God's Thumbprint the previous day, was that I'd be hiking the horseshoe ridge that I'd seen from my shelter. The ridge was superb, with a wider than normal path, fewer roots to negotiate, a dry pack, and clear skies. I was also aware, from my nightly guidebook reading, that the next 50-odd miles were relatively flat. That merely means that there were no major climbs. There were always ups and downs on the trail, but on this stretch there was nothing too strenuous over an extended period of time.

The available shelters were either too close—at ten miles—or too far—at 24 miles—so I set my sights on VA615. That made it a 15-mile day, and I hoped to be able to find a few other people to camp nearby. I suppose this established me as a bona fide stalker. Luckily, others had picked the same target. I ended the day in a pretty glade, just past the gushing Laurel Creek, on the north side of the road. There were about a dozen tents set up when I arrived, though plenty of room for me.

I was starting to prefer these places—despite the glaring absence of a privy—to shelters. They somehow seemed more authentic, and I noticed that people came together to talk out of choice, rather than the forced proximity in shelters. There were several downed trees to sit on, so I prepared dinner with a couple nearer my own age: Songbird, and her husband, By Pass. Songbird had been named for her proclivity to burst into song for no apparent reason, while By Pass had indeed had a heart bypass, only three months prior to getting on the trail. Her joy, and his dark humor, drew me to them. They were also avid nature watchers, calling everybody's attention to a porcupine as it scampered away from our camp the following morning.

I happened to hike out of camp behind them the next day, and Songbird took it upon herself to brush up my nonexistent flower-spotting skills. We were still wandering for much of the day through the Green Tunnel, with few flowers, though many were starting to bloom sporadically. Songbird showed me Mountain Laurel, with the delicate upturned white flower in the shape of a bowl, and several rhododendron with their vivid purple and pink flowers, along with a few others.

When she spotted and pointed out a Lady Slipper, apparently named for its resemblance to such a piece of footwear, I simply didn't see it. All I could see was the striking similarity to the aftermath of that uniquely male experience, when a doctor surgically removes a man's ability to make more babies. Lady Slipper may well have been the botanist's choice, and it was clearly a prettier name, but I would only ever see that lovely flower going forward as Vasectomy Surprise.

My botany lesson took place on a very steep climb. As a consequence, I was grateful not only for this infusion of knowledge but also because talking with Songbird took my mind off the struggle to cover the two miles uphill to reach the top of the ridge. It was one of those hills that looked far easier on paper than it did when hiking it. To my chagrin, this happened far more times than I would have liked.

Once on the ridge, most of the rest of the day was spent at a good clip. We covered almost 20 miles to get to Jenny Knob Shelter, even though we did have something of a hiatus after about seven miles. There were a bunch of hikers around me when I emerged from the trees. The trail led down to a road on which no blaze was clearly visible. Two or three of us headed up a bank, only to find a dead end. Below the bank, on our right, was a small road, US52, while far below us, to our left, was a terrifyingly noisy I-77.

Realizing that the bank had taken us the wrong way, I pulled out my phone to record the error in a video. Racewalker, with whom I'd shared the cabin at Chestnut Knob Shelter, appeared over my shoulder, fiddling about with his backpack in the trees behind me. Once I had stopped the recording, I noticed that he had actually been digging a hole in the ground, into which he was about to make a personal deposit. Not wishing to witness this private moment, I quickly retreated and returned to the road below. He told me later that I must have missed him divesting himself of his shorts by about five seconds. Such scant regard for the proprieties of everyday life was one I came to embrace, though I was happy to have missed out on this occasion.

Back on the road, a double blaze was spotted, so I started to cross the interstate, via a bridge. I was shocked at the noise, but aware that such noise is endemic in any urban environment. I had led a very rural existence in recent months. Realizing this was as much a shock to the system as experiencing the difference. I believe I was having this very thought when I turned left after the bridge, heading up a steep road. Eventually, noticing that a white blaze hadn't appeared for about half a mile, I concluded that I'd taken a wrong turn, cursed at myself, then headed back down. Disproportionately annoyed once more, I rejoined the A.T. and plunged back into the forest.

With just 30 miles to cover in two days to get into Pearisburg, I felt sufficiently comfortable the next day to take a couple of short detours. The second of these was for another dip in a water hole; the idyllic Dismal Falls.

I'd hiked up and over Brushy Mountain with Jay—or Beans—who I hadn't seen for about 400 miles, back near Franklin, NC. We were hot, sweaty, and very grimy, so a swim was an attractive proposition as we headed off the trail for the falls. As usual, the water was freezing cold, so my quick dip was exactly that. I headed in slowly—with my shoes firmly on my feet after the Laurel Falls debacle—then threw myself under the water. I emerged from the testicle-shrinking cold within two seconds, cursing loudly, before heading back out.

I had run into Beans a few miles back, at Trent's Grocery, a hiker's haven just half a mile off the trail, on VA606. Trent's was renowned as the perfect place to stop and tickle your burger or pizza habit. It was also, apparently, a great place to camp, shower, or launder your clothes. I was only stopping for a burger, though several others stayed for the night. Of course, once I reached Trent's, my hiker hunger kicked into full gear. I had not only a double cheeseburger but also chili cheese fries and a chocolate milkshake. They hit the spot, and I rationalized that they were giving me the fat and calories that everybody seemed to be urging me to get. Even other hikers had noticed how much weight I was losing, so I had started to take my calorific intake more seriously.

Wapiti Shelter ended a 14-mile day. It was located in an open clearing with plenty of tenting space. The shelter itself was something of an oddity on the A.T., for it was the site of a double murder on the trail back in 1981. Even more bizarre, the perpetrator, Randall E. Smith, was paroled in 1996, after 15 years behind bars. Clearly not deterred by this spell of incarceration, he went back to within a short distance of the shelter to try it again. This time he shot at two guys, one of whom he had known from his schooldays. Both men survived. Smith was put in jail to await trial. Four days later, when an officer brought him his evening meal, Smith was found unconscious. Attempts, which I would have suspected were perfunctory at best, were made to revive him. They were unsuccessful, and Smith was dead at 54.

Beans and I hiked intermittently with one another the following day. At one point, while I was by myself, I passed through Big Horse Gap, which was a small, deserted forest road. Just beyond the road, I was making my way through some very tall ferns, with a few chipmunks chittering away nearby. In an instant, everything went deathly quiet. It was as if a velvet cloak had descended upon the forest. A few seconds passed, then I heard all sorts of noise in the dense undergrowth to my right. Something was moving through the forest, very fast, and couldn't care less who knew about it. Now, I'm married to a

Puerto Rican, so I know something about exaggeration, but this felt exactly like the T-Rex part in Jurassic Park. You could hear him thundering about, raising expectation, before you saw him.

Bracing myself, armed only with my whistle and trekking poles, I waited and listened. Suddenly, there was nothing to listen to anymore. I don't know what it was, but I'll swear it was something big. I'm only glad that it decided to stay in the ferns, and not challenge me to whistle it to death. That could have gotten ugly.

A two-mile, 2,000-foot dip into Pearisburg from the top of Pearis Mountain concluded an exhilarating six days. I didn't know it then, but trouble, serious trouble, was literally just up the next hill.

Chapter 29: Pearisburg and injury

In my past life, I would have said that Pearisburg was a bit of a dump, with no redeeming features. But, for a hiker, it compared favorably with Vegas. The motel was a touch grim, but I was able to shower, sleep, and do my laundry. Even the Wi-Fi was passable. However, the real beauty of this place was its impeccable location. Our motel was within spitting distance of a Mexican restaurant that had a great bar, with a pretty barmaid, and served 32-ounce beers for $2.50. As my dear old brother Dave would say, "It's so cheap, it would be a crime not to drink it." Along with Beans and a couple of other hikers, I trusted this theory, and committed no crime.

No more than 100 yards behind this little gem was that other part of the hiker's dream, the A.Y.C.E. Chinese. How these establishments operate anywhere near the A.T. is still a mystery to me. There were several other stray hikers occupying the restaurant when we turned up, and all were contributing handsomely to the proprietor's bad day. Beans and I revisited the sumptuous buffet at least four times, returning to our table with the sort of crammed plate you'd reprimand your kids for.

It turned out to be impossible to pass the Mexican restaurant on the way back without helping ourselves to another couple of beers and a game of pool to round off a very satisfactory night.

I was at the post office as it opened the next morning, and gratefully replenished my food bag. There was no real hurry, so I headed over to the Dairy Queen for another blowout, this time of eggs and pancakes. Trigger and Shellback were there, plotting their plan for the day. We sat and chatted for a while, so it wasn't until about noon that I set off.

The climb out of Pearisburg was probably the messiest part of the trail so far. There were a number of switchbacks that appeared just to be leading up, then down, then almost back to the beginning. I heard later in the day that the A.T. was being re-routed a few days after I passed by, so I suppose not too much care was being lavished upon this soon-to-be-redundant part of the trail. The lack of maintenance certainly showed, with the path overgrown and comparatively uninspiring.

Eventually, I started to head up Peters Mountain, so I knew that my major climb of the day was beginning. I'd probably been climbing steadily for about a mile and a half when I came across an older guy, about the same age as me, sitting on a log. He was having a short break with his dog after a tough climb. As I approached them, I hailed him in a cheery voice, raising my poles in a friendly gesture. His dog leapt at me, biting me on my pant leg, around my shin area and tearing my pants. I was shocked but, thankfully, it looked as if the mutt hadn't broken any skin. The poor owner was mortified, muttering that this was the first time the dog had bitten anybody. Of course, his words were about as much use to me as a chocolate coffee pot. He clearly wasn't sufficiently mortified to offer to pay for a new pair of pants. After I had expressed my grave doubts over the dog's biting record, I left him and went on my way.

Sometimes, only a veiled, British insult will do.

My shock had subsided, although I was still shaken up. For some reason, the incident spurred me on to walk harder, and faster, than usual. It helped that I was walking along a glorious, flat ridge all afternoon, but there were no immediate prospects of a shelter. I had foolishly passed Rice Field Shelter soon after I got to the top of Peters Mountain. I initially went over to investigate. The ridge was completely open, while this shelter was set back, just in the woods, about 200 yards off the trail to the right. The place was empty when I got there. The shelter boasted the most exposed privy I'd seen on the trail, with a single sheet of plywood between it and the shelter, fully open on three sides. At that point, I decided to hike on, hoping to find an acceptable campsite on the ridge.

A couple of hours later, I was in Symms Gap Meadow and getting concerned about my sleeping arrangements that night. I was also a bit worried about my water supply, which looked tenuous, at best. Consequently, I started to look out for anything resembling a stream. This instigated my ritual of rising panic, which always accompanied doubts over solo overnight stays.

I was somewhere near Groundhog Trail, in increasingly deep and darker woods, when I was relieved to happen upon Trigger and Shellback. They were setting up in a small clearing at the side of the trail. I found an acceptable spot—almost vertical would have been acceptable to me by this stage—and we spent the evening around a campfire. They gave me some water, but I chose to drink it, forgoing a hot dinner. Instead, I prepared myself a cold wrap to eat.

It rained overnight. I had saved sufficient water for a proper breakfast so, with my concoction of oatmeal and protein powder swilling around in my stomach, the three of us set off together. Trigger and Shellback were both faster hikers than me, but I wanted to keep up with them to make sure that I gained a few more miles to get ahead of my self-imposed schedule.

We had only been hiking for about 15 minutes when I put my foot on a wet rock, which was covered in moss. I slipped heavily for my tenth fall of the trip. I landed on the rock itself, poorly cushioned by my now less-than-ample backside. As I composed myself, a slight glance to my right showed that my head was only about three inches from a jagged rock. I exhaled slowly and deliberately, then considered my position.

This felt like a lucky escape, so I told the guys to go on without me. I had proved to myself, as if proof were still needed, that the correct pace for me was my own pace, and that hiking alone was to my benefit. It was a lesson I eventually jettisoned, though that was still to come about a thousand miles up the trail.

Alone again, I pushed on as well as I could. The lack of any real substance to my previous night's meal started to impact me, and I weakened dramatically. I reached Bailey Gap Shelter at about 3 o'clock, where four youngsters were lunching before moving on. We fell into conversation while I made myself some food. After only a few minutes, I decided that my day was done at just ten miles.

In the way of most young hikers I met, they were very open people. One of them—I believe he was an Australian— spoke about various places they had visited. Indeed, they had started the hike around the same time as I had. Despite that, they had found time to take vacations while on the trail; they had just returned from a couple of weeks in Hawaii. I shook my head in admiration at their spirit and their obvious capacity to live life to the full. I felt very comfortable with them, so I asked a favor.

My phone didn't get a signal at the shelter, and I would always worry if I'd been unable to speak with Diane. The worry was more for her than for me, so I asked this team to take her number. I wanted them to call her when they reached higher ground. I asked them to let her know where I had stopped, and that I was tired, but okay. Of course, they made jokes about saying they would call her, then say "Hi Diane, Steve's dead," after which they would hang up. I believe I impressed upon them that calling a highly imaginative Puerto Rican in such a fashion wasn't an especially good idea. I think they got my drift.

Diane told me later that she didn't believe them when they called, accusing them of covering up a serious illness that I obviously must have. You may have gathered by now that my darling wife's default position is to panic. She will always look at the worst side of every conceivable situation. Nevertheless, they were eventually able to convince her after a while, so all was well.

I slept that night with a strange feeling that I couldn't quite articulate, but one that had me thinking that I was about to enter a critical part of my hike. On this, I was spot on.

All my concerns of the previous night seemed overblown the following morning. The day dawned bright and clear, and the forest picked up that mood. Suddenly, everywhere was teeming with life. Rodents of every description put in an appearance, despite my previously unimpressive wildlife tally. I walked through an area in which there must have been 20 different animals, with mice, squirrels, and chipmunks all competing for my attention. At one point, right in my path, something stuck its head out of the undergrowth only to immediately withdraw it. I couldn't identify if it was a snake, a chipmunk, or a rat, so quickly did it move.

All this new life, along with reports from other hikers that they had started to see bears regularly, took me back to my first few days on the Appalachian Trail. Every tree stump and burned tree looked like a potential bear, while every tree root up ahead on the trail had to be examined as to whether or not it was a snake. None of them ever were, of course. As time had gone on, I had ceased to think about such things, although this focus was now back. I spent the day hiking purposefully, but warily.

I eventually settled for the night, after about 15 miles— and another small credit—at Laurel Creek Shelter. The first six miles of the day, once I'd moved uphill from my shelter, had been along another spectacular ridge, followed by a fall and rise totaling about 4,000 feet.

I was coping very well with the climbing at this stage, and getting more and more positive about my chances. I rationalized my previous night's malaise as just one of those things, chalking myself up a mental credit for coming out the other side. These small victories on the trail, which may appear so trivial to others, were immensely useful to me.

There were about a dozen of us at Laurel Creek Shelter, either inside or set up in tents. It made for a lively evening, and I went to bed in much better spirits.

Hanging my food bag had become a matter of routine for me by now. Frankly, I didn't pay too much attention to the bag's contents, because there always appeared to be an unlimited supply of everything I needed. Pulling the bag down the following morning, I noticed vaguely that it felt a tad light. It wasn't until I opened it that I realized that I might have something of a logistical issue.

People had continued to express concern over my weight loss. I had been squeezing more food down my gullet without noticing this rapid depletion of my supplies. Opening my bag for breakfast at Laurel Creek revealed that I was down to my last two protein bars. The discovery was more than a touch concerning, as I wasn't due to resupply for a few more days, and I hadn't let Diane know what I might need.

Checking my guidebook, I hoped that if I could get to VA621, Craig Creek Valley, I might be able to persuade the owner of the Four Pines Hostel, Joe Mitchell, to come and pick me up. From there, I wanted Joe to take me ahead on the trail to his hostel, where a grocery nearby would allow me to get more supplies. The second part of the plan would be that he would then shuttle me back to VA621 the following day. From there, I would slackpack back to his hostel, then stay with him for a second night. The fact that Joe also shuttled his guests to and from Homeplace—an extraordinary A.Y.C.E. restaurant, with real southern cooking, served family style—also played into my calculations.

I started the 14-mile day with this plan firmly in mind. At the top of Sinking Creek Mountain, I found a signal on my phone to call him. Joe was great, and we arranged to meet at the crossing at 3 o'clock. The target seemed to be eminently doable, given that the mountain incorporated what looked like a ridge for the next five miles, followed by an easy climb down to the road. Of course, on the trail the terrain makes all the difference.

The rocks were becoming more pervasive, so I started scrambling a bit to make sure I could meet this deadline.

At around midday, I ran into a young guy in a long flowing robe. He was using a carved wooden staff as a hiking pole, and walking barefoot. Somewhat counter-intuitively, he had the trail name of Noah. I would have thought Moses was more appropriate. He was with a young woman, more traditionally attired. We had a brief chat, mainly about his lack of footwear, and I was just about to head off when I heard the unmistakable rattle of a pissed-off snake. It was a timber rattler. In the absence of any intention on the snake's part to clear the path for us, I took the opportunity to pull out my camera to record the little tinker rattling away. I was simultaneously thrilled and a tad frightened. There was apparently no immediate prospect of him clearing a path for us, so the three of us plunged into the undergrowth, passing him at a distance of about six feet before rejoining the trail.

I was later told that such snakes tend to wander around in pairs and are often about six feet apart. I had been provided with another fine illustration that knowing hardly anything kept me from worrying too much about details. Had I been aware of this at the time, I would have plotted my course more carefully. God knows what Noah would have done. Mind you, with a name like that, maybe he had a direct line.

I got to the meeting point with ten minutes to spare. At precisely 3 o'clock, Joe's girlfriend, the delightful Debbie, showed up and offered me a beer. Call me old-fashioned, but that is never a bad quality in a woman.

Debbie drove me to the hostel, which was a huge converted garage that smelled of sweat and far too many other bodily fluids for my liking. I decided to set up my tent in Joe's field, along with about six or seven others. After a quick shower, about ten of us piled into Joe's van, and headed to Homeplace. Here, we filled our boots on fried chicken, country ham, beef, mashed potatoes, green beans, baked beans, biscuits, gravy, and coleslaw. There were five hikers at our table. All of us filled our plates three times before staggering to the van, which Joe had sportingly let us use. On the way back, we did a quick detour to the village shop to resupply, then headed back to Four Pines for an evening of cornhole. This simple little game involved lobbing a set of beanbags onto a propped-up board, some 30 feet distant, then letting them slide up the board into a pre-cut hole.

Playing cornhole with Joe should be avoided at all costs. He is so good at it, and he kicked our collective butts all evening. He supplied water, soft drinks, and even beer, but only charged for specific shuttles. He told us that a donation, entirely secret and at our own discretion, was all he'd like us to consider. I know that most hikers don't have a great deal of cash to throw around, and that Joe's openness and trust could have been abused. A number of us spoke about this. We all concluded that this wouldn't be the case. I am sure everybody carried through and left at least $10 each. Joe's was a great place and, with my pack now replenished, I looked forward to the following day, which was a Sunday.

It was to prove the worst day on my trip so far.

Chapter 30: The injury kicks in

I'd been picked up by Debbie about 16 miles short of Four Pines, so I had a great opportunity the next day to complete those miles with only a few items in my pack. I was able to leave my tent—along with most of my belongings—set up in the field. Joe lent me a small day pack for some water and a few snacks, as well as my water filter. Debbie returned me to the place she had collected me from the previous evening, and I set off.

It was a revelation. I stormed up the first climb, Brush Mountain, in great time. I even passed a few people, a rare event in itself. My far lighter pack, not surprisingly, made a huge difference. I was now extremely fit, so the climbs became a joy, not a struggle. I made a mental note to do more slackpacking in the near future.

Even better, at the top of Brush Mountain, I ran into the delightful Sprout, a 2012 thru-hiker. She had set up her own Trail Magic session, bringing hikers breakfast burritos and Coke. She had reached this beautiful spot via an approach road. I sat and chatted with Sprout and a young Swiss couple who had joined us, for about ten minutes before heading on. I felt so good that I really wanted to relish my hike and the day ahead.

About 400 yards further along the ridge, there was a monument to Audie Murphy, one of the most-decorated American war heroes. Audie had died in a plane crash on this mountain, and the monument was appropriately at or near the site of the crash. He was also somebody of significance to me.

When I was young, my dad and I used to love watching movies, especially Westerns. Dad use to refer to them as "Cowdies and Indibums," in those unselfconscious, pre-political correctness days. Audie Murphy had turned to Hollywood after coming home from his wartime heroics and made a few of these films. Dad and I ate them up, and Audie was one of our favorites.

It was a surprisingly moving monument, and I felt that it was a wonderful spot at which to place it. I had laid my pack, my hat and, I think, my glasses on a bench, while I took the opportunity to read the inscription and look around. I know that Audie is more popularly revered as a military man, but those few moments had me thinking back to my dad and those Sunday afternoons in front of the TV. We'd have the sound turned down low as my mum slept in her armchair.

My day had started so well, but it was from here that it went dramatically downhill, figuratively rather than literally, and made me re-think my entire hike.

With thoughts of my dad and Audie bringing a few tears to my eyes, I continued along the ridge with renewed vigor. I was soon heating up with an accompanying sweat. Not wanting to stop, but needing to cool down, I grabbed both my hat and my bandana with my right hand. I swept them upwards while I maintained my pace. Immediately, I became disorientated. I realized that my glasses had gone, as well as the two pieces of headgear. I wear progressive lenses, with the upper part of the lens far weaker than the reading part. For that reason, my longer distance vision wasn't too bad, though certainly imperfect. I quickly retrieved my hat and bandana, but was searching for my glasses when the memory of the monument popped into my mind. I recalled, or believed I recalled, seeing my glasses next to my pack. With no real thought, I turned and hurried back to the monument.

It was much further than I expected, so I must have been motoring after leaving the monument. By the time I got there I had a sinking feeling that they weren't going to be where I had imagined them. Worse, it seemed certain that they were, in fact, back where I'd removed my hat. There was nothing on the bench and nothing nearby, so I had to retrace my steps once more. I tried to estimate the distance I'd traveled but, of course,

I was looking for a needle in a haystack. I never saw those glasses again.

Now, if this was all that happened, it certainly wouldn't have been an insurmountable problem, more an inconvenience than anything else. I called Diane and let her know what had happened. After she had commiserated with me, I moved on, determined not to let this setback ruin my day.

As an aside—and I swear I'm not making this up—about ten miles further on from the monument, I passed through the somewhat aptly named Lost Spectacles Gap. I let out an appropriate curse, I can tell you.

Many miles back in Damascus, I had bought a brace for my knee. I bought it more as a preventive measure than anything else. However, I didn't wear it for longer than about 20 minutes before deciding to rely upon ibuprofen as an alternative. For some reason that I can't recall, I had decided to wear the brace on this morning, and the knee felt fine. What was suddenly much more alarming was an increasingly sharp pain in my shin. I felt it shortly after I had given up the ghost on my glasses. The pain came on every other step. I was soon in a lot of trouble, for it deteriorated rapidly.

Even though I was carrying a light pack, the hike became progressively more difficult as I headed towards the infamous Dragon's Tooth. I was scrambling over rock after rock, and really putting my left leg through it. To add insult to injury—or in this case, to add injury to injury—I smashed my head into an overhanging branch during this miserable climb. Another visceral curse alleviated the immediate pain, and I felt that the hiking gods were trying to undermine me. It is strange to me how paranoid I became when things went wrong.

Dragon's Tooth was a huge, 40-foot-high rock at the top of a mountain that provided wide views over the entire valley. On a normal day I'm sure I would have climbed the Tooth to take in the views, but I was ready for my day to be over so that I could rest my leg. The real difficulty of this feature wasn't the Tooth itself; it was the dreadful descent after the Tooth, with the need to scramble down treacherous rocks. I found it to be absolutely awful. I started to realize that my adventure could well be over, with my leg dragging more and more. Had I felt fully fit, I would have attacked the climb down, but I arrived back at Joe's with a sinking feeling that I was done.

Naturally, my hunger hadn't diminished. So, my impending finish notwithstanding, I joined my ravenous fellow hikers on another pilgrimage to the previous night's A.Y.C.E. extravaganza. As I sat there, with everybody around me laughing and passing around plates heaving with ham or mashed potatoes, I couldn't help feeling desperately sad that I might be going home.

It wasn't that I didn't want to see Diane—far from it. It was more that I had learned how to do this. I didn't want it taken away by something that I couldn't understand or identify. If I'd simply decided that the hike wasn't for me, then that would have been okay. But that wasn't the case. I was good at this. I'd learned self-sufficiency in a way that surprised me. I'd come through the various difficulties, and even indignities, that every hiker faces, and hadn't been found wanting. My leg was a mystery to me at this stage, and I truly didn't know what to do. So, I took more ham and more mashed potatoes, laughed with the others, then got on with what was in front of me, right there, right then.

With limited choices, you take the ones open to you.

Sometimes we know what we need to do before we accept what we need to do.

In the morning, having slept well and convinced myself that my leg felt better, I went through my normal routine. When everything was packed, I headed out of Four Pines, then down the road to the point at which I'd emerged from the forest the previous evening. The trail crossed VA624, then dived back into the trees. It then headed up and over the fabulous MacAfee Knob, across Tinker Cliffs, and along several ridges before emerging at Daleville, the next town. I had really been looking forward to this section.

The trailhead was only a short distance from Four Pines. Walking slowly along the road, I was having all sorts of conversations with myself. Was it over? Was I up to this challenge? Would I be able to walk off the pain? For, by now, I knew that the pain was there to stay, and that something nasty was happening to my leg. Getting dressed in my tent that morning, I had noticed a redness on my shin that hadn't been there the previous evening. The trip to the trailhead had already taken its toll on me and, for one of the first times in my life, I listened to what my body was telling me. I considered my options.

I could try to hike for two days to Daleville, which was about 25 miles away through a testing wilderness. The alternative was to take the easy way out and hitch a lift there. Once there, I could seek some medical help. I was starting to hope that I had shin splits. If it was just that, a couple of days resting in a motel could get me back on track. However, my pessimism had returned, telling me that it was something more serious. There was only one realistic answer, so I stuck out my thumb. As things transpired, I may well have put my life in danger if I'd tried to brave it out, or "been stupid," as my wife put it so succinctly, later.

A guy pulled up within minutes, with two hikers already on board. He was taking them to the Dragon's Tooth. I asked him if he could take me to a more hiker-friendly road so that I could thumb a lift into Daleville. Once he'd dropped the other guys off, learning that what I needed was a hotel, he offered to drive me to Blacksburg, Virginia. He told me that there were plenty of hotels there, as well as an urgent care center. I gratefully accepted his suggestion.

The drive was about 25 miles, so I was quickly out of my comfort zone, with the A.T. rapidly receding in the distance. I had no idea how this was going to play out, but, in my heart, I thought it was very likely over.

I asked my Good Samaritan to drop me at a Starbucks in town, where I would normally treat myself to a triple, grande, non-fat latte. On this occasion, I went for the full-fat version, positioning myself as far from human contact as possible. I'd showered at Four Pines but hadn't been able to do any laundry, so my clothes were well beyond critical.

There was a convenient hotel a few blocks away, and I made a booking over the phone. I preferred not to give them an opportunity to see me before they accepted me. Sometimes, discretion truly is the better part of valor. Once I had the reservation, it might have proved tricky to reject me on the grounds that I resembled a homeless person. As a result, I checked into the Comfort Inn Suites later that morning. I accepted with a smile the disapproval of the desk clerk. After some emergency laundry, I got a cab and headed over to the urgent care facility. The guy who had brought me to the town had offered to run me around if I wished, but I didn't want to impose upon his good nature any more.

After ordering an X-ray, the doctor spent a while examining my leg. She soon determined that I didn't have shin splints, eliminating a blood clot at the same time, which I hadn't even considered. We talked about my hike and, when I mentioned that I'd been bitten by a dog several days previously, I was only doing so in a conversational way. She looked closer at the spot in which my pants had been torn. After a lengthy examination, the doctor told me that there was a break in the skin, and that it could easily have been caused by the dog. That concerned her even more. She pointed out that the left leg was swollen and red. In fact, she said that the redness appeared to have spread since the examination had started, some 20 minutes earlier.

The doctor told me that she was pretty sure that I had cellulitis, a bacterial skin infection. She impressed upon me that this was a potentially life-threatening illness and that, had I proceeded to Daleville, I may well not have made it. There is nothing like an imminent death warning to concentrate the mind. I asked the doctor what my options were. She said that I should rest for about ten days, complete an antibiotic course, then see how I felt. When I looked at her with an inquiry on my face that said *get real,* she became a tad more realistic: "Try to keep your feet above your head for the next couple of days, rest and take your pills, then see how you feel." That was more like it.

A nurse gave me a strong antibiotic injection in the butt. Then, she prescribed a ten-day course of pills, with a vigorous warning to take seriously my instructions to rest for the next couple of days.

Chapter 31: Back home

I left the urgent care center and returned to my room with a bunch of conflicting emotions fighting for my attention. Setting myself up on my bed, with a pillow elevating my leg, I took a deep breath, then called home.

Diane listened patiently while I told her what had happened at urgent care. She made it clear that, in her opinion, I'd be better off at home. I think she had already moved on from the hike; the only issue for her was getting me better at home. To her credit, she didn't push things, and she left the decision to me. I let her know that the doctor had told me that I should be okay by Thursday, only a couple of days away. I neglected to tell her the part about ten days' recuperation. I thought it might muddy the waters a touch and get her on my case, when I didn't want to have that conversation. I was on the verge of being forced off the trail by an injury. I needed only positivity at this stage. I placated Diane sufficiently to see how things worked out in Blacksburg, but I fell asleep that night in a grim state of mind.

When I woke, I felt a lot more comfortable, though I couldn't actually test the leg, other than to hobble to and from the bathroom. On my first visit, there was some pain. Gradually, that started to subside, and I grew hopeful that the antibiotics were working their magic. However, the day wore on and, knowing the challenges that the trail presented, I grew increasingly pessimistic as to a return, not only on the Thursday but at any time in the future. Hikers often chatted about leaving the trail, then trying to come back. I'd been convinced that if I'd gone home, I would have quickly and irrevocably slipped back into that other life. This life, the one I'd been living on the trail as Mighty Blue, would be immediately gone. For me, previously a non-hiker, returning straight to the trail on Thursday was my only realistic opportunity to complete this adventure.

So you can only imagine my disappointment on that Wednesday morning at the end of May—two months, four days, and almost seven hundred miles into the hike—when I opened my eyes. I could both feel and see that things were worse. The leg looked angrily red and hurt more than at any time before. As I lay there, I sighed heavily and dropped my chin to my chest. It was over. I'd never be coming back. I'd impressed most of my friends and family, as well as myself, with my resolve. Ultimately, it hadn't been enough.

While I would look forward to seeing Diane again, I knew that this would be a blow from which I'd take a long time to recover. I'd learned a lot about myself on the trip—not least, how badly I smell after five days in the woods. My goal had remained the same, and was now exponentially more important to me than ever. It's funny how important something can become when you are in danger of losing it. That was a life lesson learned and certainly retained.

I've always been a person who has discussions with myself, trying to rationalize positions I've taken. Often, I would make counter-arguments to convince myself one way or another. It was a feature of my psyche that had been sharply honed on the A.T. Over the next couple of hours that Wednesday morning, my thought process shifted from one of defeatism to a plan of action to get me back on the trail.

I'd read more about cellulitis the previous evening. I was concerned that a diagnosis from a doctor in an urgent care facility wasn't quite what I needed for such a potentially cataclysmic infection. I wanted my own doctor to look at me, do some tests, cure me, then send me back on my way.

With my plan in mind, I set about putting it into action. The nearest airport was 40 miles away, at Roanoke. There was a flight from there that took me back to Tampa, via Charlotte, so I made the decision to buy a return ticket. My reasoning was that it sent a positive message, if only to me. The cost was only $150 more than a one-way ticket, and it would give me a target date, the following Thursday, for my return to the trail. None of this reasoning played especially well with Diane. We had a slightly tricky conversation on the phone once I'd made the booking. She thought that I should only get a one-way ticket, but she knew me well enough to know that my mind was made up. Despite her reservations about my return, she agreed to collect me later that evening at the airport in Tampa.

I even calculated that my return home, plus my enforced rest in Blacksburg, would only increase my target mileage per day by less than one mile. With my confidence returning, I wrote in my blog that "a fully fit Mighty Blue will wipe that extra out every day by getting up 30 minutes earlier." Looking back, speaking about myself in the third person was a little unsettling, yet I remember feeling that I'd be on the trail again. That felt good.

I booked an emergency appointment with my doctor for the following morning, then found a cab prepared to take me to Roanoke. I set out at lunchtime to make a mid-afternoon flight. For the first time in a couple of months, everything went to plan, and I was hugging Diane later that evening at the airport, glad to be home.

The following morning, my doctor, after expressing shock over my rapidly diminishing physique, told me that she believed the diagnosis of cellulitis was accurate. She also noted that the skin had been correctly treated by the strong antibiotics I was given in Virginia. However, she was concerned that the pain persisted. The swelling and redness had disappeared, and that should have alleviated much of the pain.

Consequently, with the knowledge that I was planning to return to Virginia the following week, she ordered several blood tests. She wanted to determine if the infection had totally gone, or if it had spread to the blood or, more worryingly, the bones. My doctor required a blood culture, as well as other tests, so I had my blood taken. I had to wait for the result of the culture, which was due to be ready after the weekend.

The other possibility that she wanted to eliminate was a stress fracture, for that may not have shown up on the X-ray taken in Blacksburg. To that end, she scheduled an MRI for later that afternoon. All this was going far too well. She wanted me to rest over the following three or four days, icing both the shin and the knee every couple of hours. I could start walking more extensively after the weekend. She also gave me the sound bite that I most wanted to tell Diane: if everything came back well from those tests, the doctor was confident I'd be fine to resume the following Thursday.

So I felt that I was as good as fixed. That's more than I could say for Diane.

When I referred to Diane's parents earlier, I touched upon the way in which they had taken over her and, by extension, our lives. I had noticed this when I met up with her in North Carolina. However, the effects upon Diane only manifested themselves, as far as I was concerned, when I returned to Florida that week.

We had often spoken over the phone on the subject of her folks. I remember being particularly concerned when she, in a moment of complete frustration at her situation, wailed "I wish I was dead." I could hear her mother admonish her in the background, but it was terrible to hear how difficult the situation had become.

Returning to Florida, I could see how the intervening month had taken a further toll on Diane. She looked haggard and unkempt. She had never used an iron since I had known her; I was the one who had taken on that role in our family. She told me once I'd been away for about three weeks that she had resorted to wearing golf shirts and shorts, because they required no ironing. All her ironed clothes had been worn.

But un-ironed clothes couldn't explain the change in her or, more importantly, the change in our relationship. She was now strictly on a schedule that took her out of our home for three hours every morning, then three hours every afternoon. This was seven days a week, come rain or shine. That punishing itinerary was only broken if one of her sisters could stand in for her from time to time. Even then, she would often accompany her sister to help out.

It looked to me that she had surrendered her own life to the all-consuming lives of her folks, so my return immediately came into conflict with that. I am not blaming her at all, by the way. I, too, had experienced change. The entire week I was at home was characterized by misfires in our attempt to renew our relationship with one another. I had difficulty articulating the change when I was home, although I thought about it on my return. I concluded that we were both, for that short period of time, interrupting one another's lives. To a degree, we were both resenting that interruption.

I am a bit of a creature of habit, but I was unable to get back to those old habits in the expectation that I'd soon be back on the trail. To that extent, I never actually returned home. Once I was cleared by my doctor, after all my tests came back without problems, I was mentally going away from Diane once more. It was painful to do it, and it still hurts me to think about it now. In retrospect, it probably shouldn't have been a surprise to either of us. We had been living intense, unusual lives that demanded everything from us. We were both ill-equipped to make a change to those lives in that short period at home.

I used the days at home to reconsider my pack. I left behind several items that I either hadn't used or had only removed from my pack once or twice. Before I'd started, people had tried to impress upon me the need to take only necessary items, as pack weight was of critical importance. In my ignorance, I had believed I would need more than I did. I learned the hard way. I'm pretty sure that pack weight would be the first thing I would consider if I ever did this again; it would definitely be my first bit of advice to anybody else.

My winter clothes were left behind, and I bought two new wicking shirts that would be more appropriate for the summer. Given that hiking and camping had been entirely new to me, most of my choices had worked out fairly well. But, as with any venture, those choices could be improved upon. I even left out my chair, which had been much abused by my friends at the Florida Appalachian Trail Club. I hoped that my pack would now reflect my needs and not my slightly peripheral desires.

Food was going to be an ongoing issue, so I resolved to incorporate more pasta and rice into my diet, as well as more snacks between meals. The weight loss had been startling to all, even to me. I had the opportunity to see my ribs for the first time in about 30 years. I could also see that I hadn't been missing much in all that time.

Last, but probably most important of all, I decided to ditch my MVR water filtration system. While it initially worked well, it had become increasingly slow to gather a liter of water. I'd noticed that the Sawyer Squeeze seemed to be almost ubiquitous among new hikers. Everybody adapted it by buying a bottle of commercially available water by Smart, then using the empty bottle to attach to their Sawyer Squeeze. In the warmer months ahead I was grateful for having made this change.

Diane drove me back to the airport for my flight on that Thursday. In my mind, I was already gone and happy to be so. I'd learned that a relationship needs to be nurtured. Those few days at home had been sufficient to fix my leg, but they were nowhere near sufficient to bring together two people living complex lives that needed adjustment. That would have to wait for another day. It would also take far longer than I ever imagined that it would.

A Call to Action

Thanks so much for reading *My Appalachian Trial I: Three Weddings and a Sabbatical*. I really hope that you enjoyed it and that you'll want to read the second volume. Before you go, I wonder if you could do me a favor and leave a review for me on the Amazon Kindle website? It really won't take you long and it would mean so very much to me.

Thanks very much.

Continue the Journey

If you enjoyed the first volume of my book, then you're really going to love *My Appalachian Trial II: Creaking Geezer, Hidden Flagon*. This book takes up where the first left off, with me flying back to Virginia to pursue my goal. The laughs, the falls, the difficulty, and the wildlife all increase, so get ready for another great adventure as you continue to share my journey.

One last thing

Now that I've completed my journey, I've been writing yet another book on the Appalachian Trail. This one is called *Hiking the Appalachian Trail is Easy: Especially if You've Never Hiked Before.* The good news about this book is that it is going to be the best possible price—FREE!!!

To reserve your copy, please visit my website www.steveadams.info/contact and sign up for my email list. As soon as the book is available, you will get an email with a link that will allow you to download it.

91456318R00176

Made in the USA
Lexington, KY
21 June 2018